MW00718350

Julie,
The Angels Love You!
Love
Carolyn Porter

Angel Love

Published by Empower Productions, Inc.
Woodstock, Georgia 30188
www.drcarolynporter.com

First printing: January 2007

Library of Congress Control Number: 2006909934

ISBN-13: 978-0-9711150-7-1
ISBN-10: 0-9711150-7-9

Printed in China by Everbest Printing Co. through
Four Colour Imports, Ltd., Louisville, Kentucky

Illustrations and Cover Photograph by Mande Porter
Book Design and Illustration Color by Jill Balkus
Edited by Susan Grimm

Angel Love

*Experiencing the Power and Love of
the Angels Working in People's Lives*

by Carolyn Porter, D. Div.

Empower Productions, Inc.

To those who seek to know the love, peace and joy that Angels bring into your life if you simply ask.

Gratitude

The Angels who gave me this project and have been directing it with their power and love since the day it became known to me.

The Angel Practitioners and Friends who graciously agreed to support this project by sharing their stories of angelic assistance in their life, so that you could benefit from the power and love of the angelic realm.

My Daughter, *Mande*, who has willingly and artistically portrayed the beauty of the angels displayed in this book.

Jill, who brought together the inspired ideas and created a masterpiece.

Susan, for sharing her gift of editing.

My Children—*Stephen, Deborah, Scott, Melinda* and *Mande*—and the gift of their support, friendship, and love.

Pete, for his unfaltering support, encouragement, listening ear, and guidance, and the love we share in our hearts.

Contents

Foreword

The angels must love email—as they use it so often to connect people. They can find you the perfect romantic partner or, as happened with Carolyn and me, they can bring a kindred spirit to your email box.

And all you have to do is ask! That's a lesson I've learned over and over, as the editor of the "My Guardian Angel" column in Woman's World Magazine. Every week, we receive hundreds of letters recounting the most amazing, heartwarming stories of angelic interventions and encounters.

Yet, on the day that Carolyn and I "met" online, I'd forgotten that help was just a simple prayer away. I was nervous and edgy as I prepared to teach a course I'd just developed. Years earlier, I'd loved teaching and I was always completely comfortable on-stage before an audience. But for some reason, this class had me really worried.

"Give it to the angels," Carolyn gently reminded me. "They'll make sure that you and your students have the best outcome possible." Instantly, a wave of calm washed over me as I thought, "Of course. The angels have guided me this far. They'll guide me through this next step, too."

The angels have been with me all of my life. They're with you, too.

Author and Angel Therapy® Creator, Doreen Virtue, says that each of us is born with at least two guardian angels. Some of us have many more. Though we may have never seen our angels (most people haven't), most of us have had some experience of being guided, given comfort or received a sign that told us they were there.

We pray to God; the angels always respond. They're God's gift to us and all we have to do to activate their infinite gifts is ask.

And how they love to help! In fact, it's their job to do anything they can to bring us peace. We can call on them night or day, for anything—no problem is too large, no request too small. After you've asked—through prayer, thought or in writing, wait in expectant anticipation. They'll respond, often in the most surprising and delightful ways!

And the more we acknowledge their presence—through gratitude and even conversation (I talk to my angels all day long!)—the closer they move to us, the more we sense, see and know their presence, and enjoy their remarkable sense of humor. For me, the angels locate lost keys and deliver sweet kittens to my back door. They help me be a good mother, run my business, and fix my computers! And when I ran out of gas at the top of the Throgs Neck Bridge, two of them took form to rescue my children and me. Time after time, whenever I call, they are there, to soothe and uplift, to support and rescue. And they're absolutely amazing at finding parking spots at the mall!

That's why I'm so pleased that they led me to Carolyn and that she honored me with the chance to introduce this book about them. Carolyn has a deep connection to the angels and makes a wonderful guide through their wonderful world! Her book, rich with personal stories and remarkable encounters with the angelic realm, is sure to delight—and perhaps even amaze you. More important, it's an inspiring introduction to your own development of a personal relationship with the angels.

Peace be with you.

—Amy Oscar

Amy Oscar is a Certified Sacred Contracts Consultant (CMED), Angel Therapy® and Reiki III practitioner with a counseling practice in Nyack, NY. For an energy intuition or counseling session, contact her through her website at www.asifmagazine.com

Amy is the publisher of AS IF Magazine and the co-author, with Doreen Virtue, of *My Guardian Angel* (Hay House, 2008), a book of angel stories from their weekly Woman's World column.

Introduction

Do you believe in angels? I think most people believe that angels exist, at least somewhere, but I do not believe most people understand that angels are all around them every minute of every day, simply waiting for you to ask them for help. Do you realize they will not interfere in your life unless you ask them? They will only make an exception if you are in danger and it is not your time to leave the planet just yet.

I grew up believing angels were up in heaven and that I might see them one day. I was always fascinated by their beauty as depicted in the decorations during the holiday season that embodied angels. It seemed to me that they were distant beings who only came on the scene to protect someone from harm. Never in my wildest dream did I know that angels were by my side from the moment of my birth, and before.

It wasn't until many decades of my life had passed that I became acquainted with angels. From that moment on my life has stretched and expanded in my beliefs because I gained a new awareness of the spiritual realm. I cannot imagine my life without the angels, for I literally converse with them throughout every day of my life. I receive their guidance and subsequently follow it. You see, they only give guidance from love where all truth resides, so whenever I follow their guidance miracles happen in my life! When I don't listen then I only create stress and lessons for myself. My life is now an extraordinary adventure that is truly exciting every day.

As we entered the new millennium there has been a great shift in what people want in their life. Individuals are seeking more depth and meaning to their life, their relationships, their vocation, and within themselves. This is allowing people to open to new awareness of the higher vibrations present in the realm of spirit, which reveals to them the possibility of connecting with these higher vibrations. Angels are of the highest vibrations.

This book offers you stories and truths about angels and shows you how to access angels in your life. The universe abounds with angels just waiting for you to invite them into your life. Once you begin working with the angels, your life will transform in ways beyond your present knowingness; it will expand into a life extraordinaire.

Perhaps you've felt them around you or you've seen pictures of them. Maybe you've heard amazing stories of angel intervention that saved a person's life or helped someone at a time of crisis. At Christmas we see many decorations depicting angels, and figurines of angels adorn many homes and businesses. Jewelry designs of angels are available throughout the world, and many gift shops display angel oracle cards, greeting cards, and angel decorated stationary. Many books have been written about angels. Most people would agree that angels are beautiful and they give a sense of warmth, love, peace and protection. Some religions tell stories of angels who appear as messengers to particular individuals, announcing important events. Ancient cultures and religions indicate their belief in angels through their writings and art. So it seems that angels have been with us for a very long time.

You've undoubtedly heard various beliefs about angels over the years. Some are simply myths and do not relate to truth. Many others are truth. Throughout this book I will share my experiences as well as the experiences of many others to dispel any theories that are the result of these myths. I can do this because I have been actively in the experience which makes it possible for me to authentically share these experiences. Of all the qualities a human being can have, I hold authenticity as the noblest core quality for the multi-dimensions of life, but especially when working with the angelic realm.

Common myths about angels:

♡ Angels were seen and heard only in ancient times.

♡ Angels are far away in heaven.

♡ Angels are no longer visible to us.

♡ It is blasphemous to pray or talk to angels.

♡ Angels are around now only to protect you from harm.

♡ Angels are always in white.

♡ People who say they speak with angels are probably hallucinating.

Throughout this book are many stories of angelic encounters to help you understand the power of the angels. Each story is a rendition of truth and is an amazing example of how the angels work to heal the lives of everyone who asks. The name and contact information of each person who shared their story is given at the conclusion of their story. The purpose of this book is to enlighten you with the power of the angelic realm that is available to you when you're ready to accept it. The stories simply confirm this celestial angelic power and the glorious outcomes that appear when someone's life is touched by an angel.

ANGEL LOVE

Angel Love, so sweet and gentle,
a gift God gives to man,
perfect and healing, infinitely free,
but so often you cannot understand.

The burdens you carry seem heavy indeed,
because you do not ask,
for us to help you carry the load,
making easy your everyday tasks.

A simple petition; in a moment 'tis done,
lovingly we await your call,
to guide and protect, comfort and support,
as peace spreads softly over all.

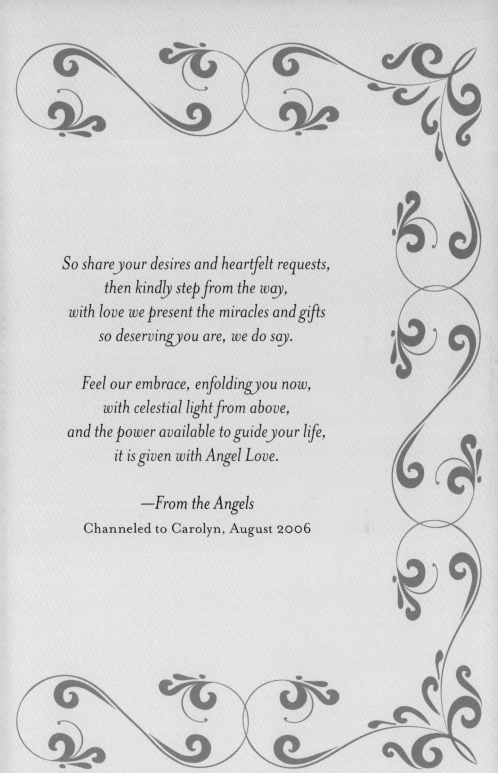

So share your desires and heartfelt requests,
then kindly step from the way,
with love we present the miracles and gifts
so deserving you are, we do say.

Feel our embrace, enfolding you now,
with celestial light from above,
and the power available to guide your life,
it is given with Angel Love.

—From the Angels
Channeled to Carolyn, August 2006

Part One

Chapter One

Angels Are...

*A*ngels are *celestial beings of light.* Angels exist in the spirit realm often referred to as heaven, which many believe is far away beyond the sky. Actually, the spirit realm is all around us and encompasses us daily, so distance is not relevant. Angels and their tremendous power are very close to you right now. An angel can seem far away but is literally a thought away. In the spirit realm there is no time or space so everything is instantaneous. When you think about this, it is pretty amazing.

Individuals who study quantum physics tell us that all living things, whether on earth or in other realms, are made of energy. Energy has no boundaries and is always connected. Energy continually travels through vibrations. You and I are therefore connected through the vibrations of energy as are all other beings on the planet, but that also means we are connected by spirit to the "other side." The other side, or spirit realm, vibrates at a higher level than earthly vibrations. This is the realm of the angels. Lower vibrations of earthly beliefs can get in the way of our connection to the spirit realm because at that level our thoughts often stem from fear which produces doubt and disbelief. When an individual breaks through their doubt, everything is possible because their vibrations will rise to a higher level of awareness. This includes seeing, hearing, feeling, and knowing the realm of spirit where the angels exist. The angels help us raise our vibration into a higher state of consciousness.

Think of the sky. As you glance upward you see endless blue with maybe a few billowing puffs of white scattered about. As you look to the horizon it appears the sky reduces to a mere slit and fades away, but if you continue walking toward the point that seems to be fading away, you will discover as you reach that place that the sky is still just as wide and glorious as it was from where you began. It's only your perception that believes the sky fades away into nothing because in reality it is the same breath, depth, and width everywhere. This is the same with your beliefs about anything in your life; it is merely your perception of what is truth.

What I'm saying to you is this. Angels are living beings who continually remain with you, particularly your guardian angels, however always remember that you can summon a host of angelic beings for any need you identify. The beauty of this is that it doesn't matter whether you believe in them or not, they are still with you. History has proven their existence with countless examples of miraculous experiences due to angelic assistance. Just as the sky seems to be ending when in actuality it extends forever, the same may be true of your doubt that keeps away the angelic realm. Open to the possibility and allow within you the movement of spirit. Let go of resistance, and all matter of extraordinary can be revealed to you.

So angels are energetic beings who are completely connected to all the energy of the universe, including you. The difference between angels and you is that they have remained in the light while you chose to come to earth. As a result, having only known love, they can only share loving expressions of a higher nature. They only impart truth because that is all they know, and they graciously and willingly await your beckoning so they can assist you in whatever you ask.

Angels have no boundaries in the realm of space or time; it doesn't exist for them. This can be disconcerting when you receive a message that something will happen soon. Like most humans, you probably see it as happening in a day or two, or at the very most a few weeks, when in actuality it may be several years working to reach you. It could be you aren't ready just yet, or are continually putting up blocks that stop it temporarily. In reality, your desire is already in front of you because everything in the spirit realm is instantaneous. Once you ask, it is given, and given immediately. If it doesn't show up for you immediately, it is because you have more steps to complete in readiness. Experiencing it before you are ready would not be in your highest interest because you wouldn't be ready to understand or appreciate it.

Angels are God's messengers for angel means "messenger of God." They exist in the presence of God and all other beings of the light. They delight in assisting you in whatever your needs are, but they can only help you if you ask them to help. Angels act as an intermediary between the heavenly kingdom and this earth. Angelic messages are always from love and angels express their love with encouragement, support, miracles, comforting, guiding, applauding, directing, blessing, protecting, enlightening, and above all, loving you.

Message from the Angels

There are no moments in time more important than the other, for time doesn't exist. It is man-made and creates limitations. In our world every moment is eternity and eternity is in every moment, for they are one and the same. When one takes a deep breath and dwells on that breath, in then out, time is no more. So with each breath, that is the moment of realness that has no end.

Chapter Two

Outdated Beliefs

S*ome religions believe angels* were only visible in ancient times, and Christianity speaks about angels before Christ was born and while he lived on this earth. The stories are found in the Christian's Bible where it is said that angels were reserved for very special announcements or appeared only in a time of crisis. The story of the shepherds on the hillside seeing and hearing a multitude of angels telling them about the birth of Jesus is one example, and another is the story of Daniel in the lion's den when an angel appeared and shut the mouths of the lions so he and his three friends were not harmed. There are many other stories of angels assisting in the lives of people here on earth during that time period. But often ministers and theologians suggest that angels were no longer visible, that they will once again be visible when you reach heaven.

So why do you think this would occur? Do you really believe that angels would no longer be visible for the rest of time? Do you think individuals no longer need their assistance?

My belief, which is supported by thousands of other like-minded individuals, is that angels are even more prevalent today than they were in ancient times. There are multitudes of examples over the years of people sighting angels, hearing them speak, and feeling their presence. In the turbulent times of this century, it seems people need the reassurance, peace and love of the angels even more. And people seem to be searching for greater depth in their lives as well as more spirituality. Skeptics may say these people who see, hear or feel angels are simply making it up or hallucinating, but since the number of people experiencing angels is increasing by large numbers, it seems this is not the case.

Angels are not partial to any particular religion. Many religions talk about angels and believe in their power, even though they may refer to them by a different name. It doesn't matter what your religious or spiritual beliefs are, the angels will help you. Some people worry that believing in the power of angels or talking to them is blasphemous. Remember that angels are messengers of God who bring messages from the Creator to you, the creation. They bring gifts for you with love, and they want you to give glory to God for the gifts they bring you.

Another old belief is that *angels are far away in heaven*. Heaven holds many mysteries. Because of its mysterious countenance, people can create what heaven is like according to their belief system. As a result, you may have been given the idea that angels live there and are far from us. This belief is part of the separation that some religions teach—that God and all heavenly beings exist far from earth and can never be seen until we die and go to this heavenly place.

These were my early teachings, but over the years, as various glorious experiences appeared in my life, I knew things were different from what I had been taught. As these experiences occurred, my thinking changed. It wasn't something I had planned or was even seeking to change, but once you experience something beyond what you thought possible you cannot step backward into old thinking.

As I opened to new things and quit placing limitations on my beliefs, new awareness of the spirit realm flowed into my being. I was amazed at things that were happening. At times I would feel a sudden influx of warmth when I was quiet, or feel the soft brush of something warm against my face or shoulders. I had been fascinated by angels in the past, but now the fascination became very strong.

I remember asking one time, early in my process of understanding, for a sign that angels were present around me. Immediately I felt a brush of something warm over my right shoulder and a soft movement of the air around me. I glanced over my shoulder but no one was visibly there. No door or window was open nor the heat or air-conditioning running at that moment that could create the movement of air. Because I had just asked for a sign and it came instantly, a strange feeling came over me of something beyond the norm, and I was convinced that it was an angel who brushed my shoulder and moved the air around me.

As I contemplated what had happened, I thought about space and time. If heaven was so far away, how could my request have been responded to so quickly? I remember thinking that maybe heaven wasn't as far as people had said, or perhaps angels hovered near each of us all the time. I asked for more awareness of the angelic realm, because the one thing I felt as the brush against my shoulder and the air stirred around me was peace. I felt warmth, serenity, and very special. I knew this was good.

So if angels are around us, does that mean some are near us and others are in heaven? Or do they fly back and forth? Or could it mean that they can be in more than one place at a time? Perhaps there is even a possibility that heaven is closer that we have been taught. Maybe all of space is filled with angels? And just how many angels are there? These questions continued to circulate through my thoughts. Perhaps they've circulated through yours as well.

Since energy is everywhere and is in continuous motion, and because energy is not governed by space or time, it seems that energetic beings, who in actuality are not bound by space or time, can be anywhere and everywhere simultaneously if they desire to be (or at the very least arrive in the blink of an eye). Beings not confined by physical form are therefore not limited by our earthly boundaries, so if we can move beyond those boundaries and open to spirit, everything is possible.

The belief that *angels are only around you to protect you from harm* is another fable. Assuredly they do protect you, but they offer so much more than protection. Example after example is being shared in this book to substantiate this statement. Although I am aware of multiple times my angels protected me from harm, there are so many more times they guide, encourage, support, love, and applaud me.

Many people believe angels only appear in white, that this is the holy color of heavenly beings. While it is true that white is depicted as the purest color, don't you think angels enjoy the entire spectrum of color provided by the magnificent splendor of the universe? My very first visual encounter with an angel was in full living color—silvery blue garment that glowed, long golden hair, blue sparkling eyes.

Message from the Angels

You are not far from us nor we from you. Why do you think thus? There is no space or distance except in minds of man. We are all one and when your thoughts rise higher through the realness of knowing, you can know us. We know you and seek the company of you.

Chapter Three

Connecting with the Angels

The angels wish to connect with you and await the invitation to enter your life. As soon as you ask for them to be present in your life, they are there. There are multiple ways you can connect with your angels: through seeing, hearing, feeling, sensing and experiencing their presence. Although you may be able to connect with them in all of these ways, there is usually one or two in which you connect easier and better. Understand this, working with the angels is not meant to be difficult. It is very simple and perhaps that is why so many people miss hearing and feeling the angels. We've grown so accustomed to things being complicated that if they're too simple we doubt it can be of any value or even be working. Not so with the angelic realm.

Seeing

ॐ

When you see an angel, it may not be as an actual figure of an angel, although that is certainly possible. People who see angels are what we call clairvoyant. Your third eye chakra is the center which opens your *clairvoyance*.

One night, some years ago, I was meditating in my bedroom, sitting Indian style on the floor. I was feeling very connected to the spirit realm when I suddenly could see, even with my eyes closed, a very bright light in my room. I opened my eyes immediately and there before me was a magnificent angel. Her wings were enormous with a wide span as she towered above me. She was so beautiful, and I could see her sparkling white wings but only on one side, for she seemed to be turned sideways. Those wings breathed with life and I could see every section of the wing as it folded over the next with the appearance of velvety softness. They were covered with twinkling sparkles of light. Her face glowed with a white light and her blue eyes danced in the light. Her hair was golden and flowed gracefully over her shoulders, but what amazed me was her garment. It wasn't white as I thought it would be, but was a silvery blue that shimmered and danced with prisms of light. I sat there motionless, in total awe of what I was seeing. I knew what was in front of my eyes but I also knew this was beyond anything I had ever experienced before, or even knew was possible. I felt great warmth around me. Perhaps it was the angel's warmth or perhaps it was me perspiring. But one thing I do know, I had never felt so much love and peace at any moment before then as the angel stood before me. She told me she was my guardian angel and her name is Hope. She said she was always with me and would never leave my side. Then she was gone. In that short moment my life completely transformed, and from that point I hungered to know and understand more.

A year or so later, I was working with an intuitive who saw my angel and described her to me, without any prior knowledge of this angel. The description was a perfect match to what I had seen before. Then a gifted man I had asked to work with me in a healing energy session, saw an angel by me and began describing my guardian angel Hope, the same angel I had seen and the intuitive had seen. That confirmed to me what I already knew, but I confess it felt good to know others had seen her as well. Yes, I know, this was simply a wee bit of doubt that apparently the spirit realm knew was there and helped me move past it by confirming my earlier experience.

Angels come in all shapes and sizes. They assume the form that you need to see at that time. They are not sexual beings, but can appear as a male or female presence. They take on these forms so you can see according to your realm of knowledge. I always see beautiful angels with faces that light up with the light of God. They are always smiling and project a radiating essence from their own light. Although I see some angels in garments of white, I see most of them in color, for I believe the angels love using the full spectrum of color that the universe provides. Color resonates with our senses in a most energetic way, and I think angels utilize that energy.

Angels are often seen in other ways. You may see a streak of light glide by you, like a shadow that glows with light. Some individuals have glanced up to see an angel bending over an ill person in a hospital bed as if comforting him, or you may simply glance up from reading a book and there before you is a beautiful angel.

Have you ever seen spots of light? They look like the spots you see when a camera flashes, twinkling like stars up in the night sky. These spots could be white or colors, and could be seen anywhere around you. These are angels, and it is the energy of the angels that you see. Doreen Virtue calls them angel lights and what a glorious way to describe them, for they are beings of light. They often appear in white—it is suggested that these are guardian angels—as well as green, blue and purple. Of course any color can be seen, for angels use every color of the spectrum. It has been said that the colored spots are those of archangels. This may be primarily true, but I continually see my guardian angels in colors as well as white. (Yes, you can have more than one guardian angel, and often do.)

I have seen these twinkling angel lights for years, but until I learned that these were angels around me, I thought it was something abnormal with my eyes. Others have shared they also thought their eyes were having problems. It's quite comforting when you see these angel lights because you know the angels are nearby, watching over you as they wait to help you.

One time I was having trouble sleeping. I got up and was sitting in the dark in my den. I did some breathing exercises and some tapping on various energy meridians to relax my body and mind, and I talked with the angels around me, asking for help to quiet my mind so I could sleep. In a short while I began to feel sleepy so I stood up, and headed toward the bedroom in the dark. Ahead of me on the floor were several streaks of white light, kind of wafting along the hallway floor. I knew it was my angels and I laughed softly at seeing them below my feet. I asked them what they were doing on the floor. The reply was that they wanted to get my attention and they knew I'd be looking down to watch where I was going since it was dark. How clever I thought and as I glanced straight ahead I saw the same streaks of light in the middle of the room. I heard one say, "Is that better." I just chuckled to myself and was grateful for their humor and companionship. I drifted off to sleep with a big smile in my heart.

How Do You Open to Your Clairvoyance?

First you may need to cleanse your third eye of blockages and heal any imbalance. Call upon the Angels of Clairvoyance to assist you as well as any other angels to help. Be sure to place the intention of seeing more clearly from genuine love and desire in your heart. Simply say "Angels, please help me to cleanse and purify any areas that are blocking my psychic vision." Then say "Thank you" and you're ready to receive. Do not block the process by doubts because that in itself can block you from seeing clearly. You may need to do further cleansing as well. It could be advisable to ask the angels to help you uncover the blocks. You might want to journal their answers or simply pay attention to what you see and hear, always trusting in its validity.

Hearing

Many instances have been shared by individuals or even groups of people hearing angels. Some have reported hearing a rushing or rustling sound, as in the movement of their wings. Many have heard words and phrases given quietly in lovely soft whispers. At times, when being alerted for danger or if they want to get your absolute attention, their voice may be loudly heard. You might hear the sounds of beautiful music that sings to your heart, or you might hear their voices inside your head. Ask them a question and sit quietly. An answer will come to you, perhaps with words or an inner sensing of the answer. *Clairaudient* is someone who hears the angels.

A friend and I were spending a few days at a beach along the Florida coast a few years ago. We always walked on the beach at night, enjoying the quiet and lack of people. School had started for most of the country so the condominiums were partially vacant. The night before we had lain on our backs in the sand and looked up at the stars, breathing in the spectacular view. We were speechless as we experienced the unifying of our souls with the universe in this vast display of magnificent beauty. Our goal was to relive that experience again on this night.

As we were walking down the beach, kicking our feet through the water's edge, I began hearing a voice telling me to go back. I ignored it at first, thinking I couldn't be hearing that since we were on a mission to once again experience the gift of the stars. But I heard it again a little louder and I felt my heart begin palpitating at a much faster rate. I had a panicky feeling churning deep inside me with a knowing that we were to move quickly, so I turned to my friend and said, "We have to go back. I'm being told to turn around and do it immediately." My thought was that possibly someone was following us or maybe watching us and we were in danger.

As we approached our condo and I reached in my pocket for the keys, I became aware that I had forgotten the keys, a very unusual behavior for me. This was a privately owned condo so no one in management would have a key except for housekeeping, and they were long gone for the day. We glanced around the condo and noticed a light on in a nearby dwelling. I knocked on the door, explained out situation and asked to use a phone to call a locksmith. The older *couple and their two friends gladly helped us, and although it took a while for the locksmith to get to us, we were finally in our condo. In hindsight I realized that if we had lingered on the beach that older couple could have been asleep or gone somewhere and we wouldn't have had anyone to help us. The angels are wonderful and we were so grateful for their protective warning.*

I personally communicate with angels throughout my entire day. I ask questions, ask for guidance, and ask that they stay with me throughout the day. At times I've asked for a sign to indicate their presence. They always respond. It could be with a flow of words or I may feel a deep sensing of the answer. An email may pop on the screen with information about something I asked them, or a song begins playing on the radio that has words that give me a new thought or idea. Life becomes such an amazing experience when you allow the angels to enter your life.

How Do You Open to Your Clairaudience?

Our ears are the instrument for hearing the angelic messages. We must clean them periodically as they become clogged with the sounds of our earth, often based in fear. When we hear painful or unhappy things, our ears are then dirty. Try going out in the sun and asking for the energy of the sun to cleanse your ears, or simply ask the light of God to filter through the debris and cleanse your ears so you can hear the realm of spirit better.

Feeling

Many people simply feel the angels. It could be a sense of sudden warmth around you or even a sense of being wrapped in angel wings, like a wonderful embrace. Sometimes I've felt as if someone is brushing against my back or shoulder, or a gentle brush across my face when no one is in the room with me. There could be a moving of the air or movement as if a soft breeze has stirred. Some people get a whiff of a fragrance, perhaps a favorite of a relative or friend who has passed on. The aroma tells you they are close by and then you begin to feel their presence. When you feel angels you are considered *clairsentient*.

One time as I was working with a client with the angelic realm, I began to smell cigarette smoke. No one was smoking in the room or even in the building, but the smell was definitely there. My client began to laugh softly and upon inquiring as to why she was

*laughing, she shared that her grandfather was a smoker.
As soon as we recognized who was connecting with us he
shared a couple messages with my client.*

Angels often use a fragrance of something familiar
as a sign that a spirit is nearby and wishing to connect. The fragrance often is the sign to help you
open to and feel the connection of the spirit.

Sometimes I simply feel their love within my
heart. I sense their presence or have been asking for
them to be near when I'll feel a contraction or tight-
ening of my heart that sends a wonderful sensation
of love throughout my body. It's an awesome feeling
because it fortifies me with the knowing that the
angels are in and around my energy. Perhaps you've
felt something similar and maybe even wondered
what it was. Just the sweet angels!

How Do You Open to Your Clairsentience?

The biggest problem here is individuals not trusting
what they feel. It seems too easy so they doubt. Again,
it may be necessary to do some clearing of your lack
of trust. Ask for heaven's help to do this and genu-
inely be willing to discard your doubts. The chakra
center to open clairsentience is your heart. The key
is to open your heart and allow only love to express

through you. An expression of love is trust. Ask for help in opening your heart wider and wider so you can erase your doubts.

Knowing

You may be going about your life when out of nowhere a new idea or thought appears in your mind. You're thinking, "Where did that come from?" You mull it around in your mind and realize it's a very good idea. Perhaps you begin smiling because it's such an awesome idea and it came to you just like that. Maybe it even changes your life in a most euphoric way. This is from the angels! They love to help you with ideas and possibilities, but then leave the choice of whether or not to do anything with it to you. Since you have complete free will, the choice is always yours. But they are very happy when you use their ideas because they know those ideas can transform your life. If you have this knowing of angelic presence you are referred to as *claircognizant*.

So many people share how they simply know something. They have no explanation how they know, they just know the answer. Maybe it's a feeling about some future happening which does eventually happen. You experience one of those "gut" feelings that doesn't make sense, but you pay attention and later discover it was a truth. Individuals often experience an inner nudging that they ignore, but sometimes that feeling continues to bother them until they listen.

I can assure you that becoming a public speaker was not on my list of possibilities. However, some years ago I began getting messages to become a speaker. Customers in our health store would tell me I should be a speaker and friends said this as well. But the mere thought of it made me tremble. I decided this was ridiculous because there was no way I could ever get up in front of an audience and speak. I went on with my life. Some months went by, and a continual nagging thought surfaced that said I needed to become a speaker. I became restless and frustrated as I could not see myself speaking, ever. But the message continued and finally, one day, I simply gave up the "battle" and told my messengers, "Okay, you win, I'll take the speaker training." You see, a customer in our store taught a speaker training and had mentioned I should take it several times. And you know what, on some level I had a knowing that I could do this.

So I took the training although I was a so petrified when I arrived that my clothes were visibly shaking. But then something amazing happened. I discovered it wasn't as bad as I thought it would be and by the end of the training I no longer shook. I had broken through the fear and had found it better than I thought. Now speaking is easy, so I'm grateful for the angels keeping after me. They knew this was good for me to do, even though I didn't agree initially. This choice has allowed me to experience things I would have never experienced if I hadn't listened. They knew I knew this about myself but was simply ignoring it because I focused on fear.

A knowing may be just a sense of something, perhaps not to proceed according to your intention or take a particular road.

I remember hearing a woman say she was driving down the expressway and knew which exit to take since she traveled this way frequently, but on this particular day she drove right past it. When she realized what she had done she was irritated since now she would have to backtrack and probably be late for her meeting. However, later that afternoon, she learned of a horrific traffic accident in which she would certainly have been involved had she traveled her usual route. She knew the angels kept her thoughts elsewhere so she forgot her exit.

How Do You Open to Your Claircognizance?

Once again, lack of trusting your "gut" feeling will block your claricognizance. Everyone has these "gut" feelings but so often discount them and sweep them under the rug so to speak. They do this because they don't want to do something or doubt they can, so they ignore the nudging—all from fear.

Releasing the fear is essential for you to know the truth within you. This also involves the heart chakra, for in opening your heart to more and more love, you know the truth that resides within you. The knowing you are experiencing may not make sense and you may not understand how you can know it, but you do. Listen and follow that knowing.

Message from the Angels

It is without knowledge you know. It is within your soul and cannot be learned, only remembered. The flowing from your soul is the truth that sets you free and opens the channels of all holy thoughts to reverence you. Only believe the truth within you, not without you.

Chapter Four

Experiencing the Angels

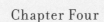

$\mathcal{M}$ost people experience angels through one of the above mentioned methods more than any other. While it is certainly possible to experience angels in all of these ways, one or possibly two become your usual experience. It might also be that as you open to higher awareness of the angelic realm, the manner in which you experience them may change. Anything is a possibility!

Here's an example of experiencing angels. You're tired and upset and feeling like the world is caving in on you. You want to cry until there are no tears. Without warning a feeling of great warmth slowly envelops you and a surge of energy rushes through you. This is experiencing your angels. Of course every time you encounter an angel and receive their assistance, you are in essence experiencing them, no matter what manner of experience it is. I remember a situation that was without any doubt an experience with my angels.

I had been out running a multitude of errands and had another place to be in a short while, but was presently heading home for a bite to eat. As I neared home I realized I had forgotten to stop for gas and my tank was almost on empty. I don't usually forget things like this and being a new car I wasn't sure how much gas I had left—I'd never let it get this low before. After grabbing a bite to eat I headed out again, but before I went even a mile the light came on indicating I was low on fuel. I started to feel some panic because there was no gas station for about ten miles from where I was. So I simply asked the angels to help me. I explained my situation and that I needed enough gas to get to the gas pump. I kept driving and a few minutes later I glanced down at the gas gauge and received quite a surprise. The needle on the gauge had jumped up to the next highest line and the light was no longer on. I had heard of things like this but had never experienced it myself. I kept looking at the gauge thinking my eyes were playing tricks on me, but it always read the same—one line higher. And it remained at the higher line all the way to the gas station. I laughed out loud as I realized how silly it was to have even a moment of concern with the angels around. They are amazing!

Perhaps you've experienced a situation in which a tragedy was nearby but you avoided it miraculously. Something out of the ordinary happens and you have no explanation that makes sense. Avoiding an accident as was mentioned previously is a good example of angels present and protecting. You sense there is a problem, maybe that something is wrong at home, so you immediately head home to find someone needing assistance. You were experiencing the presence of your angels. We often refer to these as miracles, and indeed they are. You might see them as "gut" feelings, and indeed they are. Your expenses have outdone your income one month and you ask for divine help. Out of the blue Aunt Sally decides to send you an unannounced check or you receive an unexpected refund. Again, feel blessed for the presence of your angels.

Message from the Angels

Your world is a beautiful place, but its beauty is often missed. Human eyes look elsewhere thus seeing destruction and chaos. But there is purity and love surrounding the world and could easily reach every soul if they lifted their eyes a little higher. As the rainbow shares its beauty after the storm, so are we prepared to spread beauty to the eyes who can truly see.

Chapter Five

Inviting the Angels In

You Must Ask

*T*his is the most important part of using your angels. You must ask for their help. God and the angels already know your needs but you have free will so they cannot interfere in your life. The only exception is if you are in grave danger and they prevent you from leaving this planet before your time to go. So if you want to communicate with the angels and God you must invite them into your life.

You can petition them to help you by merely thinking the thought. The thought alone will bring an angel instantly to your side. You might only think "Help" without even saying the word angel, and they will be there immediately. Some people say the words out loud, perhaps like a prayer. There are no rules in the realm of spirit so whatever works for you is perfect with the angels.

There are no time constraints or lack of any kind in the realm of spirit. This means you cannot wear out an angel or ask for help too much. Neither will you pull angels away from helping others since they can be in many places simultaneously. The angels will help you with anything you ask, big or small, so don't refrain from asking because you think it's too trivial and would be a bother. They want to help you with everything; in fact, they delight in helping you. Their desire is for you to be happy and at peace.

Receiving Your Desires

The first step in receiving the desires of your heart is to know what it is you want. Most individuals know what they *don't* want, so it's vital that you define what you truly do want. I suggest you make an actual written list, like a wish list. At the very top, as a header to your list, create a "thank you" statement to the angels, maybe something like this: Thank you angels for working out all the details of my wish list so that my desires manifest into my life with ease. Read this list over and over to remind yourself that the fulfillment of your desires is in motion the minute you ask for it. Then take it a step further by envisioning a team of angels preparing the details as you sit back, relax, and watch.

Here's the "catch" that can stop it dead in its tracks, and is the variable influence that affects the end result. Resistance! What do I mean by resistance? Doubts that your desires will ever manifest. Thoughts and words that say the opposite of your statement. Deciding you'd better do something to make it happen. Here's what happens. You made a positive intention of what you wanted. But then you began to doubt and thoughts crept in that were defeating. That's a negative. What happens if a negative charge (lower vibration) hits a positive one (higher vibration)? Nothing. Absolutely nothing. You have succeeded in stopping your desires dead in their tracks.

Here's an example of stopping it dead. You've been nudged to write a book by that little voice within you. The thought has come through many times and you're mulling it around in your mind. You imagine how it would feel to have people reading what you wrote and have your book on the bookstore shelves. It feels good. So you began researching for information on this process, particularly on how to get started. You have been intuitively given the topic and it was suggested that a notebook be purchased for you to keep with you at all times to gather notes. You begin.

But the notes aren't fitting together, at least that's the way it seems to you, and you're unsure if the topic you were given is really good. You're beginning to doubt. Your enthusiasm is declining and you let days go by without working on it. You think of all you have to do in your life with not enough time to do it all. Then you think of the many books out there and decide no one would probably read it except your family and friends anyhow. The notebook is filed away for a rainy day sometime, and your dream went out the window because you are blocking it with your own negative thoughts. This is actually self-sabotage.

But what if you asked the angels to help you gather good thoughts and ideas, allowing them to work out the details? What if...you asked the angels to help you with time and your negative thoughts about your lack of time? What if...you surrendered the entire dream and allowed it to flow to you effortlessly? You might be amazed at the results, for this is inspiration, or being spirit-led. And inspiration requires internalizing the desire so that you actually feel the manifestation of it before it has materialized, which is so much more than just a thought in your mind. My books come in this way. An idea jumps into my thoughts or sometimes I actually hear the title. I simply say, "Sure, I'd love to write that book," and the words seem to magically appear. In fact, as I was in the process of attracting the perfect stories for this book, I was getting a little concerned at the beginning because not many stories were appearing. I remembered my own words about surrendering the request and asking the angels and God to take it over, so I did this. That same day stories began to appear and continued until time to end the collecting of them. And they came effortlessly from places I could never have orchestrated myself!

The whole point of what I'm sharing is that you can have whatever you desire, but the only way it can manifest is if you get out of the way. Simply define what you want, ask for it, internalize the feeling of having it, and let it go as you patiently wait for it to appear. Sound simple? It is simple, but not easy to implement since humans by nature want to do it themselves. And while you're waiting for it to appear, be sure to say "thank you" since you know it is coming. This is called faith and is a prerequisite when interacting with the realm of spirit. Faith is simply unquestioning belief in what has not been seen as yet.

Each day petition the angels to help you for every project, every task, every step of your daily routine. It's beneficial as you begin your day to take a few moments and ask your angels to help you throughout the day. Try writing a list of items for that day perhaps in a notebook designated for angel requests, and watch everything on your list manifest for you. Here's a sample of a list I used one day.

♡ Today I wish to spread love and light to everyone with whom I come in contact.

♡ As I am writing further in my book, I ask that you provide the perfect words flowing effortlessly from Divine Inspiration.

♡ Thank you for the abundance that allows me to pay my bills today. I intend for the abundance and prosperity in my life to continue.

♡ I am grateful for the clients I have today and ask for Divine wisdom to share what can be most beneficial to their life. Continue to send me individuals who desire the guidance I offer that can change their life for the better.

♡ Thank you for assistance with my computer project today, making it easy to implement.

♡ I surrender this day and ask that all of my activities raise me up into greater awareness of my highest good.

♡ I am asking for additional angel stories today for this book. Thank you for sending them, especially since this is really your project!

Within an hour of asking and being grateful for additional angel stories, two appeared in my incoming emails. Several new ideas flowed through that day—Divine inspiration—that I included in this book. Everything I asked for, and was grateful for before it was even here, showed up!

Communicating With the Angels

You want to communicate with the angels but don't know how. You've read or heard various ways to connect but it's not working for you. I'll share some ways to communicate easily with the angels.

♡ *Don't try to force the communication.* First you must know you cannot force the communication. Demanding or feeling frustrated will simply delay the connection. All you do is simply ask, wait, and listen.

♡ *Quiet your mind.* This may feel like an impossible undertaking with all your mind chatter. Like most in life, don't give up. As thoughts enter your mind, acknowledge them then let the thoughts go. After a while, your ego will calm down and you'll become quiet.

♡ *Play soft music.* The angels love music and it seems easier to connect with the angels when soft music is playing in the background. It also helps you get quiet and open to receive their messages.

♡ *Light a candle or burn some incense.* This also seems to help create an easier connection with the angels. Perhaps it is because of the relaxation it brings to you or maybe allows you to move beyond your thoughts with more ease.

♡ *Sit in nature.* This is a powerful way to commune with the angels. Nature is the breathwork of God and resonates with the higher vibrations of the spirit realm. You can find all answers in nature as well as communicate beautifully with the angels.

Message from the Angels

We never leave your side. If your eyes would open wider you would see us. It is our wish for you to call upon us for the smallest to the largest task. It is easy for us so we make it easier for you. That's what we mean when we tell you to let go of things. It's only then we can lift your burdens and help you enjoy your life more. We long to help you, so do ask us.

Chapter Six

Angel Hierarchy

*T*here is a hierarchy in the angelic realm with nine choirs of angels. They are divided into triads. A triad is simply a group of three that blend together or are placed one over the other. Although all angels can impact our lives, each group is designated for our support in certain areas. It isn't necessary to know or understand any of the hierarchy because when you call for angelic assistance the ones standing by to help you will answer. However, I was guided to include mention of their hierarchy to give you a greater knowledge of their realm.

In the Old Testament of the Bible that Christianity adheres to, reference was made multiple times to the Seraphim and Cherubim. These angels guarded the holy temple according to Biblical translations and are the highest order, ranking most important in God's host of angels.

Next there are the Thrones followed by the Dominions, Virtues, and Powers. The last three levels humans use the most and are the Principalities,

Archangels and Angels. A brief chart that follows can simplify this for you.

There are countless stories of guardian angels; even movies and TV specials have been created around this theme. So let's clarify the thoughts surrounding the idea of a guardian angel.

I believe, as do many other like-minded individuals, that each of us has at least one guardian angel that is assigned to remain by our side during our lifetime. Their main task is to assist us in living a life surrounded by our dreams, one that is happy, peaceful and full of love. But again, they cannot offer assistance unless we petition for it. They never leave our side from the moment of our birth. This always makes me a little sad that I didn't know this until many decades later.

I also believe, and I share this belief with many, that we can have more than one guardian angel. Is it because we need extra help for our life or perhaps that we have much to do while here and need the extra assistance? For whatever reason, I have met three guardians of mine. Hope is the first one that actually appeared to me as a way of introduction to her existence; I shared this encounter earlier in this book. She is a magnificent angel and is the "first in command" so to speak. Others have seen her as well which simply confirms to me her presence around me. She's a very strong and powerful angel, yet very loving. Months later I became acquainted with Angelique, a totally different looking and acting guardian angel. She's more light-hearted, smaller in size, full of energy with bouncing hair and a "go have some fun" attitude. Only recently, years later, I began to feel a male essence around me and inquired as to who was with me. That's when I met Mercor, my third guardian angel. He is apparently guiding me in business and with understanding men in a new way, sort of a different aspect of life in which I apparently need additional assistance. I've also experienced several spirit guides assigned for specific undertakings and one expressly for the healing sessions with my clients. It's so much fun as well as exciting to know they are with me every day and guiding me in all different situations of my life.

Know this: You have at least one guardian with you at all times. Why not begin by inviting this angel to enter your life and your consciousness now.

I also invoke the archangels consistently, using the one that serves my needs at that moment. Archangel Michael is extremely powerful and stands ready to help you with any issue, but particularly ones that involve fear. The archangels can be present in many lives simultaneously, so you and I can be using them at the same moment in time. I also call upon ascended masters for assistance. I suggest you reference the writings of others to learn specifics about these angels and masters. Some suggestions are listed at the end of this book.

Highest Triad

Seraphim Choir One	♡ Highest order of God's angels ♡ Humanitarian and Planetary assistance ♡ Angels of pure love, light and fire
Cherubim Choir Two	♡ Angels of harmony and wisdom ♡ Divine protection and knowledge ♡ Can function as personal guards—guards religious temples
Thrones Choir Three	♡ Angels of justice and will ♡ Relationship and planetary issues ♡ Creates and sends positive energy

Middle Triad

Dominions Choir One	♡ Angels of intuition and wisdom ♡ Meditation, arbitration assistance ♡ Assists leaders in churches and politics
Virtues Choir Two	♡ Angels of movement and choice ♡ Healing through elements—earth, air, fire, water ♡ Known as the miracle angels

Powers Choir Three	♡ Angels of space and form ♡ Protection and defense assistance ♡ Keep track of human history, oversees home and family

Lower Triad

Principalities Choir One	♡ Angels of time and personality ♡ Leadership, problems, discrimination issues ♡ Guards continents, countries, cities—assisting global reform
Archangels Choir Two	♡ Angels that rule ♡ Each archangel has different attributes ♡ Can belong to several levels—enjoy human contact
Angels Choir Three	♡ Assigned to humans, including guardian angels ♡ Transformation, death, birth, protection ♡ Guardian angels can communicate with all other angels.

Message from the Angels

Love descends on everyone, filtering through the fragments of the earth. It is warm and beautiful and seeks to penetrate the soul, yet many turn away. We continue to send love that graces the world so that cosmic warmth will reach into hardened hearts and melt the walls around them. Love softens and helps to create a smile.

Chapter Seven

Are the Messages You Hear from the Angels?

I remember this was a very definite challenge for me when I first knew I was hearing the angels. How do I know that what I'm hearing is truth and not just my own self-talk? How do I know if it's an evil entity?

So often, in the beginning of opening to the realm of spirit, communication comes from the angelic realm but the person doesn't hear it. The angels really want to help you and will give you what you ask, but if you're busy looking for a particular answer or a certain preference you may miss the answer entirely. Your perception is very narrow compared to the angels who can see from such a higher vibrational frequency. They have no boundaries of perception as you do. Your communication could come through an email message, hearing the soft voice of an angel, the words from a song on the radio, a billboard, a person in line at the grocery store, or a feeling that sweeps over you. Notice the thoughts that come to you or the feelings you sense once you ask for their help. Your answer could be in what you feel!

Anything the angels share with you comes from a place of love. They will never tell you what to do. Instead they guide you with suggestions that propel you on your life purpose if you ask. They will never ask you to interfere in anyone else's life for that person must learn from their own experiences. Everything they tell you will inspire you in some way. Stay receptive and the messages will come. Relax. Breathe. Listen. They want to communicate with you and it is you that must remain open to receive the messages. Their messages will begin as *you* or *we*, never the singular *I*.

Signs That Angels are Near

We've established that the angels always answer you, but if you tend to be the skeptic, you may want confirmation that they are indeed supporting you. Here are some ways they offer confirmation of their presence and their assistance. Every one of these named below I have experienced.

♡ *Chills*—someone is sharing thoughts with you and immediately you know internally this is an answer. Chills run through your body and you know this is good.

♡ *Fluttering within your stomach*—like butterflies when you're excited.

♡ *A candle flame* suddenly flickers or gets larger but there is no draft.

♡ *A feather* appears, or even multiple feathers—they visibly show up.

♡ *A butterfly* glides by or alights nearby, even perhaps on your body, or perhaps a bird.

♡ You find a *coin* or *multiple coins*, often on the ground in front of you.

♡ *A fragrance* wafts through the air, maybe the smell of fresh roses, even though you have no roses in the room and the windows are closed.

♡ *The repetition of numbers*—seeing the same number or set of numbers at least three times. It's a message that says they love you and are with you. It also means pay attention to your thoughts and make sure you think about your desires and not your fears because you will attract what you are thinking about.

♡ *Repetitive ideas* that continually appear in your thoughts.

♡ *A rainbow*—all is well even though there was a storm.

♡ *A feeling of warmth* gushes through you without any external cause.

♡ *Angel lights* appear as a reminder of their presence.

Important to Remember:
The Angels Always Answer You!

So how do you know what you are hearing is from the angels and not some form of evil? Everything you hear will be inspiring, uplifting, encouraging, and from love. Angels focus on your capabilities and inner gifts and continually encourage you to step into your potential. They offer assistance in this endeavor and give you ways to improve everything in your life. Nothing they say is ever negative in any way; never do they sound upset with you. They may at times admonish you but always in a loving tone. I personally do not see any evil entities as has been described by some. I see vibrations from ego as a lower vibration that does not raise the person to a higher plane, and is therefore negative.

The biggest obstacle of hearing the angelic messages that I've encountered in my work is simply the doubt an individual personifies. If that person simply asks for clarity and realizes that the angels always answer them, the messages will be more easily heard. Doubt and disbelief are what keep the angelic messages from reaching you. When you believe, you receive!

Message from the Angels

Precious are the days and nights of your life, counted as gifts of great magnitude. Neither bought nor bartered, they are a gift for which is worthy of thankfulness. But many waste the days and nights with unnecessary vorticals that do not touch their soul. The days and nights then do not count for worth and are quickly gone.

Chapter Eight

How the Angels Help You

*H*ere's an example of how the angels helped at one point in my life.

In 2004 I was guided by my angels to place my house up for sale in late fall, close to the upcoming holiday season. Everyone knows this time of year is the worst time to sell a house, and I had expected to do this in the spring. I ignored their nudging and went on with my life. But they kept after me and I finally said "Okay then, I'll put it up for sale." When I asked who I should use as a realtor since I knew about 10 of them, I was surprised at the name that popped into my mind. "Her, I asked?" The answer came back "Yes," but I had no idea why. It certainly wouldn't have been my first pick.

The holidays passed, people came and looked, but no contract. I wasn't receiving any negative feedback either. My finances were not in the best state at that time so I was looking to downsize, thinking I had to

do this. However, in February, after not finding any houses in the downsized price-range that I liked, I received the message during meditation that I was putting limits on my situation by saying I had to downsize. This puzzled me because I knew the state of my finances. But the angels insisted I need not downsize and could very well upsize. I trusted the angels' guidance completely so I began looking for a house with a higher price tag.

Still no contract and we were now into May—6 months. My realtor was upset that she couldn't get my house sold and would lament the situation, but I simply told her to have faith because when it was the right timing it would sell. I was wondering why I had to put it on the market in November though, since it hadn't sold. I couldn't find any house I liked either. Every time I'd find one the lot would be ugly or something else not acceptable. But I kept trusting the process and knowing there was a bigger picture from what I was seeing.

The end of May, I was sitting with my younger son who had made my unfinished basement into a workshop where he created wonderful objects, and he was mentioning he didn't know what he was going to do when I moved since I no longer wanted a basement.

Suddenly, a thought flew into my head—what if he bought the house? I verbalized that thought and it was as if a light went on. He said, "Mom, that's why your house hasn't sold; I'm supposed to buy it." And he did!

Of course I went out and immediately found the perfect house in an area I hadn't looked before, and it was an upgrade. But one might ask why I was instructed to put the house up for sale in November if it was going to take so long to sell?

Here's what I felt was the reason:

♡ I needed to remove the limits I had placed when I said I needed to downsize—my perception.

♡ I needed to release the house and let it go completely in my heart—many good memories.

♡ My son needed to be ready to make the purchase— always part of any equation.

♡ I needed to branch out in another direction to find my house—I was limiting the area.

♡ I also was able to be an example to my realtor as she watched me remain calm, peaceful and confident it would sell at the perfect time, in spite of her anxiety about such a long selling period—sometimes seeming delays may be for the other person as well.

The angels knew what was best and by allowing them to lead me the end result was better than I could have ever planned myself. Here are some ways in which angels may help you.

Angels Protect You

Undoubtedly you've heard dozens of stories of how angels have protected individuals from harm and danger. There are many times you have been protected and probably didn't even know it. Near misses, narrow escapes, injuries that don't materialize, illness that escapes you, miraculous healing that you cannot explain; these happen every day everywhere. Like magic, you are spared! That's the way it is; the magic of the angelic realm has protected you.

I was driving back to Atlanta, Georgia from Chattanooga, Tennessee. It had begun to rain quite hard and I was in the middle of evening rush hour. It was difficult to see due to the downpour. I had only been on the road about ten minutes when the guy in front of me hit his brakes. Of course I had to do the same and I began hydroplaning, swerving to the right and then the left, totally out of control. Cars were all around me and beyond the right hand lane I remembered seeing a ditch. It happened so fast I had no time to even think about what could happen or even how to manage the car, but as I glanced around me after my car straightened, I had managed to slide between cars and not hit anyone. There was no logical way to explain how I had missed all the cars that surrounded me. It was nothing short of a miracle and I smiled because I knew my angels had protected me. Normally I would have begun trembling after realizing what could have happened, but I felt totally calm, as if I was being embraced, so I simply said out loud, "Thank you angels."

I was feeling the peacefulness that angels bring to you in spite of my near accident. I remember thinking how calm I was and I would normally have been shaking from the realization of what could have happened. The rest of the trip home was uneventful and quite pleasant. I knew there had to have been many angels around me during that experience.

Angels Encourage You

Humans by nature get discouraged. It may be difficult to continually hold your head up high when
everything around you seems to be crumbling.
Maybe you lost your job or your spouse decided to
walk away. Perhaps you're unhappy in your work but
don't know how to escape. Maybe your finances are
not in good shape and you're struggling. Has a loved
one or friend left this planet and you are grieving?
I've been in all of these places but have learned how
to step out of these seemingly negative situations so
that I can make lemonade out of the lemons.

It's really simple to do; just not always easy to
implement. Here's the secret. Start being grateful
for everything—the job you lost, the partner that
decided to leave, the financial struggle, even your
unhappiness. You see, those things become a great
teacher for you. You have a choice—to step over it
and become stronger, or wallow in it as a victim.
People that have had great victories had to first climb
over the challenges. There are many athletes who
have stories of breaking the barriers. Think about
Christopher Reeve, remembered as the super-hero
Superman. His challenge was incredibly difficult
but he didn't let it stop him. He never gave up his

determination to walk again. Think of the great model he was for so many, especially his children.

I can remember times when the incoming dollars were less than the outgoing dollars. Ever been there? I was trying hard in my new business and living totally moment to moment. One day I was beside myself to receive an answer to my dilemma. Here was my solution.

I went into my bedroom and sat quietly on the floor. There were tears for a few moments until I was quiet enough to realize the power around me. I simply poured my heart out to God and the angels, even though I knew they already knew the entire situation. As I sat there I went through my whole story—how hard I was trying, how I didn't understand why things weren't happening, how I was doing what I thought they wanted me to do, and how I was so tired of living in this place of struggle. I knew in my heart this wasn't the way to live but couldn't figure out how to change it.

As I sat there in the still moment, I could feel the presence of God and most assuredly the angels. The room became warm and I felt as if I was melting away somewhere. I was cognizant of a protecting love surrounding me, like a warm embrace. My thoughts began to shift. I began remembering all the times in the past when things looked bleak, and in every instance my need was supplied. Then I thought of all the situations when I didn't know which way to turn, and a solution suddenly appeared out of nowhere, effortlessly. I slowly began thinking of all my blessings, all that I presently had, and realized that the only things that really mattered were already mine for eternity. I know the angels were redirecting my thoughts into this place. Suddenly everything shifted within me and I realized how blessed I was while knowing everything would be fine as it had always been. At that moment I surrendered my problem and uttered a prayer of thanksgiving for everything I had, knowing that I already had all I truly needed. I ended by saying "thank you for taking care of me and for the guidance that is coming to show me what I'm to do next." I could hear the angels telling me everything would be okay. I was completely amazed at the shift within me—no more worry or feeling of being beaten down. I finally understood what it meant to live in the place of enough, which is simply abundance. Amazingly, some new thoughts and direction came to me within minutes of my surrendering, and the money I asked for showed up in some rather unusual ways, always in time for whatever deadline there was. The angels were all around me and I know were overjoyed that I finally got it!

Angels Help You and Others Heal

We live in an amazing time of great healing possibilities. The power available to us is on a plane far above our carnal knowledge, but if we tap into that power, miracles of healing can occur. Healing of this higher vibration cannot be explained nor comprehended according to the minds of men.

You've probably heard of examples when someone heals just before their scheduled surgery, so the surgery is scrubbed. Or perhaps an individual is given a diagnosis that indicates complete healing cannot occur, but it does. A miracle? Most assuredly they are. And you can believe the angels had something to do with it. By focusing on the belief that you can heal creates an entirely different vibration that attracts more of the same. It is in this space that healing can manifest because it has raised up your vibration to a higher level. Focusing on the illness and its symptoms keeps the individual in a lower vibration where healing is difficult and very often impossible. Simply ask God and the angels to raise your thoughts into a higher awareness of vibrant health, and they will help you.

Some years ago I was working with a 70 year old woman with multiple serious health challenges. Her medical prognosis was dismal to say the least. She had chosen to try some alternative health treatments and began introducing wiser dietary choices as well as working with energy and the angelic realm. We were in a session on this particular day and of course I had called in the angels and particularly Archangel Michael to assist me. As I was clearing energy blocks so that her energy began flowing more easily, I began to feel an intense tickling sensation inside my left foot. I began moving it around on the floor in the attempt to stop the itching. It wouldn't stop. As it became more intense and was beginning to distract me, I was guided to ask my client if she was feeling anything going on with her left foot. She immediately replied that she had a tickling feeling inside and was amazed as she hadn't felt anything in that foot for the last six years, due to surgery for her rheumatoid arthritis that had fused together her toes and parts of her foot.

A moment later, a bit overwhelmed with what was going on that day, I was guided to tell her to move her toes. This wouldn't normally be medically possible with the fusion she had experienced six years earlier. But the power of the spirit realm far exceeds the power of the medical profession. She was able to flex her foot slightly and several of her toes began to move, very slightly. It was a miracle indeed and she was

*joyous beyond what I had seen in her previously.
From that time on, she was able to move her toes,
and they even improved a little more over time. So
take this advice from one who knows—never say
never because anything is possible!*

It is possible to focus your energy to help another
person. All you do is call to God and the angels
and ask that you be an instrument in sending healing to that individual. Even if they don't know you
are sending healing energy to them, they can be
healed. On some level, there will be healing.

*My youngest daughter was home from school with
the flu. She was aching all over, fevered, lethargic,
and watching TV or napping on the sofa all day.
Her boyfriend called and wanted her to come over
to his place for a while but she refused, saying she
felt too bad to move and didn't even have enough
energy to take a shower. So I decided to try working with both of our angels to heal her, or at the
very least improve her symptoms. This was also
new to me at that time and I was "practicing." I
was upstairs and simply focused my energy on her
body while sending white healing light to her body
and asking for angelic help, especially from Archangel Raphael, who is the archangel in charge of*

healing. I stayed with this for five minutes or so and then let it go. Approximately thirty minutes later I became aware of the shower water running and after my daughter emerged I inquired why she was showering since a short while earlier she felt too bad to move. Her reply was something like this. "I just started feeling better all of a sudden so I'm getting ready to go to Jim's (not real name) place." I replied that this was a fast turn around and she agreed saying that she just started to feel better. I smiled to myself and was actually quite amazed in the quick turnabout that occurred. I then thanked the angels for doing this. My daughter's fever never returned, her headache disappeared, and she went back to school the next day. Her symptoms reduced dramatically and disappeared rather quickly.

You can request protection, encouragement or peace for another. Simply put in your request as long as it comes with genuine love for this person. I've done this many times and often the person will say something about how peaceful they have been feeling now or I'll simply see a change in how they are acting and responding to their situation. You cannot interfere with another person's journey, but you can ask the angels to surround this person with guidance, protection, healing, and of course love.

What about healing yourself? Do you think it is possible? I can assure you it is from my own personal experience. If you believe you can heal yourself with the help of the spirit realm you can heal, when you're ready.

A few years ago I began having pain in one finger on each hand, the ring fingers. I thought I had strained them and paid little attention to them. But the pain intensified and the difficulties with them increased. I noticed that they would seem to stick and I'd have to literally pull them back into place. That process was quite painful. I began to ingest various supplements, thinking it was a joint problem. As it continued to worsen, I sought out an orthopedic doctor to find out what was going on. After x-rays, his diagnosis was trigger fingers, something I'd never heard of before. His solution was cortisone shots, up to two in each finger, or surgery. He said that the sheath around the joint becomes inflamed and doesn't allow easy movement when the fingers bend, thus staying in a bent position until I manually straighten the fingers. I thanked him for his information as he smiled with that look of "You'll be back." I knew right then that I would heal this.

But nothing was happening in the way of improvement, and over some months my two thumbs also developed the same problem. It was difficult to hold some items with my right hand and I noticed my hand strength, particularly in my right hand, had weakened significantly. I couldn't open jars and other things were difficult to maneuver. So I began to focus healing light into my hands while asking the angels and archangels to assist me with understanding what to do to heal this situation. Various things came to my attention to implement, like some dietary changes as well as internal blockages. I was told I was too acidic so I needed to eat more alkaline foods. Being highly motivated to maintain a healthy body and lifestyle, I was grateful to further know wiser choices to optimize my health. One day I realized the fingers weren't as painful as they had been. I was able to bend them closer towards my hand as I made a fist. More time elapsed and the pain diminished considerably, almost to no pain at all, and I could completely close my hand as I had done all my life until now. I still have times when it flares up somewhat, which simply tells me there is a block somewhere and I begin working on it.

Angels Help You with Clarity

Have you ever had the blues? Maybe you have no idea where to go in your life? What your life purpose is? What decision to make? You're feeling down and out and simply can't get yourself moving in any direction? Who better to ask for help than the angels?

As human beings we often get caught up in the do-it-all society in which we live. The message is clear that we should be continually doing something, and if we're not producing accepted results, we are failing. Not so fast. That is what society thinks, but not the way the spirit realm works. In the world of spirit there is no time and *being* is more important than doing. When you find yourself in a blue mood, it's time to get quiet and listen. State what is on your heart, and then quietly await your answer. It will come, probably very softly and unobtrusively, if you simply listen. Be patient for the timing since the angelic realm does not operate on your schedule.

I was working on my second book and doing a lot of spiritual coaching. Just before a client was expected to arrive I received an email that she couldn't come due to sickness with one of her children that had just manifested. Less than thirty minutes later a call came that another was not going to be able to make it that day—car trouble. "Okay" I thought, "there goes two. At least I have one left and the others will reschedule." Well, it wasn't long before another call came and the other client canceled completely. I bet you can guess my reaction. "What in the world is going on?" I thought. "Why all three of them?" So I was feeling a bit down and irritated because my whole day was now messed up, at least that's what I thought. I kind of moped around a bit and thought about what I should do. So this is what I did.

I got quiet for a minute and listened. Sure enough, I heard that my calendar had cleared so I could write. I was told I was procrastinating somewhat so the angels opened a day for me. Can you believe that? Those angels had done this to me! I began to laugh at myself and my response, so typical of us humans. Since I was putting off finishing the book they had guided me to write, they arranged for me to spend the day working on it. Instead of doing something to me, they had done something for me! It ended up being one of the most productive days I've ever had with writing!

Angels Help You Heal Relationship Issues

Relationships can be so tricky. As humans we are so easily bogged down in all the details of a relationship with our expectations and demands. Actually, a relationship is in your life for a very specific reason, and the other person with you in the relationship could very well be your greatest teacher. I do believe all relationships can be healed, but it won't happen as long as you're trying to do anything. Relationships heal only when you are being the love.

A client of mine was dreading a visit to her mother. I understood that feeling as that same dread had occurred with me in years past before I visited my mom. However, I learned something that changed the entire relationship and it is this: I cannot change anyone, only myself. So I set about to be the love that any relationship requires in order to be healed. I called in my angels to help me as this felt like a huge task. This allowed me to relax and simply go visit with the intention of spreading love. The result? We experienced a totally peaceful and enjoyable visit.

So I suggested to my client that she simply surrender the trip and ask for the help of the angels. I further suggested she begin seeing the trip as enjoyable and thanking the angels ahead of time for healing the relationship. When she called me upon returning, she said it was the best trip ever and it was wonderful. Not only did the relationship with her mom heal, but also with her siblings. Of course I expected this outcome when I made my recommendations, so I was delighted when she had followed my suggestions. That's always how it happens—the end result is even better than the request!

Another client was having problems similar to the woman in the above story. Hers was a bit different so I suggested she work on herself for a while. She began meditating and journaling her thoughts, and every day she surrendered her negative thoughts and asked that they be changed to loving positive ones. My other suggestion was for her to continually look for the good qualities in these family members and focus on them, even if she could only find one. She did this and before long she reported that those family members were seeing a difference in her and were responding differently to her. That's the whole idea—it's really about you and how you respond rather than about them. Take your eyes off the other person and focus on changing you, and let the miracles begin.

My boyfriend and I had a slight miscommunication. He had his view and simply wouldn't budge with his thoughts. Since he wouldn't talk to me about it I had become frustrated because I knew this would resolve nothing, but old patterns die hard sometimes, don't they? I was sitting at my computer, not being able to sleep right then, and simply talked with my angels, telling them I was giving up and for them to take over because I realized I couldn't "fix" this situation. Within 15 minutes or so, my office door opened and my boyfriend poked his head in asking if he could talk with me. I was so surprised that the situation had changed so rapidly, but even more amazed that he was awake since I thought he was already asleep. I agreed to talk of course but mentioned I was surprised he wasn't asleep. To that comment he replied, "The angels won't let me sleep; they keep waking me up. They told me to get up and talk to you and to do it right now." Love those angels! Needless to say, that taught us both wonderful lessons of surrender, patience, listening, and unconditional love; the situation resolved with ease.

Angels Support You

Angels will always support you in whatever way you need support. If you're tired of the life journey they'll encourage you. If you're doubting your capabilities they'll reassure you that you have great gifts within and to persevere in all your endeavors. If you're wavering in the direction you're going they'll give you signs of their presence. They can enable you to return to trusting the process of life they are helping to unfold with you. If times are rough financially, they'll remind you of the abundance around you that is yours by simply seeing the abundance instead of the lack.

Not long ago I was having a time of doubt, wondering if my desires would ever manifest into reality. I knew better but as a human I slip sometimes. So I was doing a little complaining. During my meditation time I asked for a sign that my angels were looking out for me and were with me. I went outside to do some gardening and was walking down the driveway when right below where I was about to set my foot was a feather. I chuckled to myself because that feather hadn't been there a short while earlier when I was walking in the same area. So I knew the angels were indeed near and again I realized how futile any doubts are. But to make sure I "got it," as I walked about 10 yards further there were two more feathers on my path. Aren't the angels awesome!

Angels Help You Find Things

This is a wonderful aspect of the angelic realm—their ability to help you find things you lose. We all do it, misplace things that is. You're in a hurry and set something down, then can't remember what you did with it. Maybe you're like me in that sometimes I hide something and do it so well I can't find it myself!

> *I remember doing that one Christmas. After the presents were opened one of my daughters remarked that she really wanted a certain item and was surprised I didn't get it for her. But I did get it. How could I have forgotten to wrap it. What a weird realization to know I had forgotten to place it under the tree. I kept looking for it but couldn't find it, so after a while I thought to ask for angelic assistance. Within a few minutes I saw the gift in a closet in my mind I didn't think of previously. Sure enough, when I went to the closet there was the gift. I smiled and was grateful again for the angels' help.*

The angels love to help you in any way they can. Next time you misplace your car keys or don't remember what you're supposed to do at a particular time, ask for their help. Remember the story I shared earlier when my friend and I were at the beach? By telling me to return to our condo we were able to find a locksmith before the evening became too late and we were stranded outside all night. It was a different way to find our keys, but it was their help that guided us back early enough to remedy the situation.

Recently I was looking for a program to load on my laptop. A couple of us were searching all through my office looking for it, turning things upside down in the search. I knew I wouldn't have thrown this away as it was costly and usable again for another computer. After much looking it appeared as if I would have to purchase another software program, something I really didn't want to do. Since it was getting late and we had to leave on a two-day trip, we had to abandon the search for then. I wanted the program on my laptop to work on various things while we were away. As we got into the car I remembered to ask for the help of the angels. Within minutes we thought of one of my daughters who may have borrowed it. I called her and she reminded me that one of my sons could have borrowed it as he had received a new computer a few months back. Ding dong, the bell rang and I remembered I had loaned the program to him and forgotten to get it back. That didn't solve my problem of using the program during the two days away from home, but I figured my angels wanted me to do other things and not work on what I thought needed to be done. I marvel at how fast it comes to us once we petition the angels help.

Angels Guide You

The angelic realm is anxious to help guide you through your challenges, but also gives guidance for your life direction. Many people hear these messages but put fear in the way and therefore discount hearing anything at all. Many individuals mention they feel they should write a book but then turn around and put up every excuse possible as to why they can't do it. That's the fear getting in the way of a Divine message. I did the same thing for many years until I began to listen to the angels and followed their guidance. They've never steered me wrong in any way. In fact, when I follow their guidance I am always amazed at the final outcome—it's better than anything I could have ever dreamed up.

I was writing a book a few years ago and making good progress on it. One morning, as I was showering, I heard a voice that said I was to put the book I was currently writing on the back burner and write one entitled THE REALNESS OF A WOMAN. *By this time in my life I had learned that if the angels guide me to do something, it's always better if I do it. So I smiled to myself and simply said "Okay," not having any idea what would go into the book. The messenger also said it would come in fast and I'd be done in three months or less.*

Wow, I thought, no rest for the weary, since my life had been quite busy of late. I really had no idea what would be in this book, but as I was driving to my morning meeting a short while later, thoughts and words began coming into my awareness. I even pulled over to the side of the expressway to write a few notes at one point. Then I saw as a problem—publishing a book costs money when you self-publish, and I didn't have any extra right then. So I asked if I was to self-publish. The answer was an emphatic "yes." I laughed with a slight sarcasm in my voice and said, "Okay, if you want me to write and self-publish this book you'll have to provide the resources to do it."

The book was completed in 10 weeks. The money showed up for every part of the process when it was needed. The material for the book literally fell into my lap. The words flowed with such ease as I typed that it amazed me. It was one of the most fun things I've ever done because I totally surrendered the entire process and let the angels guide me every step of the way. There was no stress and nothing I had to do but show up, listen, and then take the action steps they indicated. This is really what is meant by inspired—the idea grabs you and won't let go instead of you grabbing an idea and running with it. It simply flows through you.

Another way in which they may guide you is with suggestions for your environment that will uplift you. Several years ago they began imprinting on me that color and style change would be good for me. Here's what happened.

I didn't think I was in a place financially to buy new furniture at that time, but I was feeling this tug to make changes. My color scheme, left over from my past marriage, was hunter green, burgundy and cream. I accepted it as fine for the time being. But I was being guided to include sage green, many shades of purple, light yellow and splashes of red. I didn't even like red then except for Christmas decorations, so I complained at their color choices. And with a slight curtness in my tone I told them they'd have to supply the funds if they wanted me to redecorate.

I began by adding some new pillows, a flower arrangement and a little paint as the funds showed up. But I was continually nudged to venture into furniture stores to see what was out there, not knowing what I was really looking for. Nothing appealed and of course there was always the issue of money to pay for it. But one day, as I accompanied one of my daughters while she looked for furniture, I walked by a sofa set and stopped dead in my tracks. There in front of me was a set in sage green, a soft fabric, and it was on sale. But I immediately discarded the possibility since it takes money to make a purchase and I didn't have any extra. But I kept coming back to it and felt this nudging to pursue the thought of purchasing it.

The salesman mentioned they were offering no payment for 6 months and no interest if paid off by then. I didn't like the idea of doing this but felt guided to move forward with it. I bought the set on the spot and had it in my home within two days. When it was two weeks before payment was due, I reminded the angels I still needed the major part of the money so I could pay this debt; I knew they didn't want me to begin paying payments that included interest. One week later it showed up and I was reminded again of the importance of faith and trust in the power of the angels. And you know what, the color scheme the angels wanted me to use is something I really love now, and red has been added as a favorite in décor and wearing apparel as has purples. Amazing, isn't it!

Angels Want You to Have Fun

Angels love to see you smile. They are happy and full of fun so enjoy putting some humor into your day. I cannot tell you how many times I've heard the angels say to me, "Lighten up. Relax. Go have some fun. And by all means smile!"

We get so busy in our lives thinking we have so much to do that we find ourselves out of balance, in the busyness rut, wondering why we are so stressed and tense. I used to work all the time as I was getting my business off the ground. It was fun to me, not really work, but I kept forgetting to relax, smile, and enjoy life! Ever been there?

The angels want all of us to have fun because then we are happy, relaxed, and our hearts are more open. In this place our lives are more balanced, which makes our work even better after we've experienced "down" time.

In the early months of building my business I was a dedicated workaholic, often working into the wee hours of the morning. My angels kept telling me to take a break and urged me to go out into nature. But

I kept right on working, thinking I had to do this to build my business.

So one morning everything began going haywire. My internet service was out and most of my work involved using it. At the same time none of the people I was trying to reach were available. A friend of mine called and asked if I'd go to the park with her for the afternoon, making sure we'd get in a nice long walk. My immediate reply was "No, I have too much to do to be gone all afternoon." She begged, stating we'd walk, hang out at the park, relax, and go out to dinner. It sounded inviting and I thought a moment, then shifted back to my previous too busy mindset.

But suddenly I heard a voice say "Go. Go right now because your computer isn't usable anyhow." So I thought about that fact and decided to go with my friend. It was such a fun afternoon—a healthy invigorating walk in nature, conversation, laughter, swinging on the park swings, and a meal out. I was so grateful for the day which helped me realize the importance of fun in my life. In hindsight, I know the angels stopped my computer from working and had urged my friend to call on that particular day. My friend actually said something told her to call me and insist I go. Thank you angels!

As I close this section that relates to how you can invite the angels to help you in your life, I'd like to share some messages that the angels have given to a special woman named Caroline, who also shares a story in the following section of this book. She was guided to share a few of her many messages so that you too can benefit from them.

Caroline Lara's
Message from the Angels

SEE LOVE THROUGH THE EYES OF YOUR ANGELS

*When all have decided that love is important in their life,
then this is the time to call on your angels for their guidance.
They will show you how to see through their eyes. Know
that the angels are with you from the day you are born until
the day you are called home. When we start to view the
world and people through the eyes of the angels then we
start to see all in a different way. We start to notice there is
no reason to see hatred or to see ugliness. We see and
understand why situations and people are the way they are.
We then will begin to approach from a different angle. We
will become more sensitive to others feelings and needs.
Our hearts will start to open.*

*Archangel Uriel brings you the light of your Creator.
Everyone has this beautiful light, located in the center of
your stomach. The angels now ask that you close your eyes,
breathe, and raise your light all around you. Notice the
sensation you get when this is done. Know, dear children
this is your eternal light of your Creator. Ask that this light
be enlarged, then notice the love that will be poured into
you. Now, the angels ask that you spread this light to*

everyone, whether by your warm smile, or a hug. Know that when this is done you are spreading love and definitely you are looking through the eyes of your angels.

The angels ask that you now close your eyes and vision the whole world. Spread your light and encircle the whole world with this beautiful light. Now, ask your Creator to heal our world and all the people. When you decide to see through your angels eyes, you will only see total and complete "Love."

WORDS OF MEANING

Dearest children, words of meaning are the words you say from your heart. Know that when you give words of love, this is your word of meaning, when you say words of kindness this is your words of meaning, when you say words of console this is your words of meaning, when you say words of anger this is your words of meaning.

Dearest children, words are very powerful; please sit back and look at the overall picture before you speak. Dearest children, call on Archangel Gabriel to come and help you with all your conversations and communications and allow your words to be guided by spirit.

Know then children your words will be guided to speak of truth, love, and respect. Your words of meaning will then be heard and understood by all whom you converse with. Your words of meaning will have meaning. Dearest children, the angels ask that you take a second and ask for heavens help. The angels will lovingly help with choosing your words wisely.

SHINING SILVER ANGEL

A shining silver angel stands erect with wings straight up and strong. The angel stood in place and the silver was illuminating as far as one can see. She is radiant; she is so beautiful words can not explain her beauty. Slowly, she came towards me and I just looked at her. Slowly, she came closer. I was then standing in front of her. Her illumination got brighter, so much brighter, but the light didn't hurt my eyes. I asked her "What is it that you want?" She looked at me with a gaze that shot straight to my heart and I knew what she was saying without words. I knew she was here to bring me something so simple yet beautiful, and the gift she was giving me was "love". She began to move back and her light began to fade. Before she left she asked me one thing. She said "Child of God, spread this love which was given to you!"

Part Two

Part Two

True Stories: Shared from the Heart

In this section are the stories from many people who have realized the power of the angelic realm. They are ordinary people from all walks of life. Their stories confirm the presence of angels and that they really do help you when you ask. As you read these inspiring stories, understand that angels are around you right now waiting to help you. No matter what you ask of them, they can help with the solution. They are there for you just as they have been present for all these individuals who are sharing their stories with you. Call upon them and watch your life glow with their light and the miracles that will show up for you!

Note: ATP, listed with some names, refers to Angel Therapy Practitioner, a certification with world-renowned author and teacher, Doreen Virtue, Ph.D.

Angels Protecting

Listening

Years ago, my two sons and I were in a new mini van driving on a heavily traveled two lane road in the middle of the afternoon, and we had to make a left turn. There was no traffic behind us when we stopped but there was a small rise in the road. It was bumper to bumper oncoming traffic and we had to wait for an opening. The rear end of our van suddenly exploded from a truck pulling a blacktop tar trailer that hit us going about 60 MPH from behind. He hadn't even tried to stop. Because my steering wheel was slightly turned, the force of the impact pushed us into oncoming traffic. We were so close to an oncoming car (appearing that we would hit them head on) that I vividly saw the two people in the front seat brace for impact and the shocked look on their faces. My seat back collapsed and I ended up laying down when I heard a voice tell me to sit up quickly, keep my hands on the wheel, not brake too quickly, steer the car steadily, and many other commands quickly and in succession. I did what I was told and

we went through the oncoming traffic without hitting anyone, and came to rest on the opposite side of
the road berm facing the wrong way. We were all
dazed. A witness that had been in front of me had
seen the accident in his rear view mirror and had
pulled over about a half mile up the road and run
back to help. He was amazed that we went through a
narrow opening in the oncoming traffic without
hitting anyone. I could tell by the shocked look on
his face and his comments that he didn't understand
how it was possible. The van was totaled but each of
us was okay. I am sure that the voice was an angel
helping me so we could survive. If I hadn't listened
we wouldn't be here.

—Cindy Snowball
Bradenton, Florida

Schoolyard Angels

My youngest son Eric was attending a small Christian school during second grade. I always picked him
up at 4:30 every afternoon. On one afternoon I was
on the other side of town, at least an hour and a half
away. I was worried because the school had a policy
that all faculty and students were to be gone by 5 PM,
so nobody would be around to supervise and watch
over any students. I knew I wouldn't make it in time

and all the way there I prayed that Eric would not be alone and that the angels would watch over him. Eric was such a sensitive child and often afraid so I was really worried about this. I finally arrived at the school about 6 PM. Eric was sitting on the curb by himself but within sight was a lady with two kids sitting in her car. Upon seeing me the lady ran over and asked if I had a screw driver. "For what" I asked? She said she needed to force open the trunk because her daughter had accidentally left her car keys in the trunk. I asked her if her car had the button in the glove box to pop open the trunk, and said she yes, but she continued by saying the key needed to be in the ignition to do this. So I disconnected the wire in the glove box that controls the light bulb and then touched the switch that controls the trunk and the trunk popped open. She thanked me and said she had asked God for help and I came, and I said no, God and the angels made you wait so that Eric my son would not be left at the school alone. Thank you angels.

—Pete Gomez
Operations Manager and Hypnotherapist
pg7383@aol.com
Woodstock, Georgia

An Angel Appears in Bangkok

I was visiting a friend in Singapore when I decided to make a three day visit on my own to Bangkok. I set up my trip through a travel agent for my flight and hotel. I had prayed to God for a safe trip. Once I arrived in Bangkok, I saw a kiosk that offered tours for the next day. I wasn't feeling great about an airport Kiosk but I needed something. I agreed to a one day tour. Since I did not speak the language and it was such a quick trip, I felt I would be able to see as much as I wanted in three days. Just as I put my hand out to pay, I heard a woman calling my name. I turned and saw a woman dressed in white with a name tag from the travel agency saying that she was my tour agent and that she had been looking for me. I was surprised because I didn't set anything up but flight and hotel. She made the kiosk man return my money and said they had a car for me to the hotel. I told her I did not set anything up and she said it was all arranged and I was taken care of. I walked with her to meet my guide and a driver both dressed in white, and they took me to a white Mercedes to drive to the hotel. My intuition told me I was safe.

While in the car, I was feeling very safe and secure. The guide said his name, and then turned to me and repeated it translated in English, which meant

Angel. I was stunned! He went on to tell me he could be my guide for the next two days. The cost would be $40 a day. I felt that I was being protected at a very high level. After all, Bangkok is one of the most dangerous cities in the world. I was on my own and only the travel agency and my friend knew where I was in the world!

He took me to the hotel and offered to take me to the night market which I would not have gone to by myself. I was able to see and adventure all the night life I wanted with Angel since he said, "With my name badge on, no one will bother us." I felt like we were almost invisible strolling through the market, clubs and streets.

The next day Angel picked me up and we toured the floating market, the Royal Palace, had a Thai massage and toured the city. I would not have been able to navigate all the things I did without him. It was wonderful to have a guide and companion and to feel so safe. He had also been a novice monk in his youth and he shared the Thai religion with me and his beliefs. It was a wonderful gift of protection and education. I went to places I would not have gone by myself and felt totally safe along the way!

The following morning, Angel called me to tell me that his company had called and told him that I was correct that first day when I said I had not ordered or was to receive a pick up at the airport or have the opportunity of Angel as my guide. It had been a mistake. *I don't think so, I thought—divine intervention!* I took a cab to the airport to go back to Singapore and was smiling all the way. Archangel Michael has always been my companion as well as having the blessing of wonderful guides and angels with me on my life's journey. I think this was their way of keeping me safe along my way! I am very grateful for Angel and my Angels for this wonderful and safe experience!

—Nora Lee Smith, ATP

Noraangelstar@yahoo.com

Tampa, Florida

Just Ask the Angels

For as long as I can remember I have seen, felt and heard the archangels. Michael has been with me most of the time. I could always see things other people could not, not always an easy gift to have.

My daughter Tricia was 10 years old. It was a warm summer night and I had just had a root canal done five days before. It had finally reached the place where I no longer felt any pain. It was 10:30 P.M. when Tricia received a phone call from a friend of hers. I told her she was not to have her friends call so late. She talked on the phone for a few minutes then hung up and went to her room. We assumed she had gone to bed. After about a half hour my husband went up to her room to ask her something. He went into her room and found a mound of toys underneath her covers to make it look like she was there. He yelled out for me to come upstairs. I found the mound of toys and no Tricia! We were very upset to say the least! We had no clue where she could have gone and no phone numbers of her friends to call. My root canal started throbbing so I took some codeine the dentist had given me to help ease the pain. We searched through our caller ID and called the numbers that had called our house to no avail. We decided to go to bed about 12:30 since there was nothing more we could do until morning. We were pretty sure she had gone to a friend's house to spend the night since our older daughter told us she did but she didn't know which friend. As I lay down in the bed to try to sleep, I closed my eyes and suddenly saw Tricia lying dead with no clothes on in a field by our house. Everything was in clear detail and certainly not something I wanted to see! A male, about 6 feet tall and on the heavy side, was walking in the shadows behind her waiting for the right moment to grab her. I shot up in the bed and out loud I called my guides and angels and Tricia's guides and angels to have the police find her now and bring her home safe. I lay down and within a few minutes I heard my older daughter call out that the police were at the door! I shot out of bed like a bullet and ran down the stairs. I thanked the officer for finding her and bringing her home. I also thanked the angels for helping. I told my daughter how scared we were and how she wasn't to ever do this again. I asked her what she was doing walking down the street so late at night in the first place. Apparently her girlfriend's mother had a boyfriend living with her and he decided that he did not want my daughter spending the night because the girls were making too much noise. I told Tricia to be thankful she was alive because there was a man following her home and was planning to grab her. She looked at me and told me she felt that some-one was following her but she thought she was imaging it. Needless to say she never did that again!

—Cheri Dye, ATP
www.JaguarShaman.com
Bolingbrook, Illinois

Martha's Miracle

A group of six healer friends from around the country got together over the Labor Day weekend on the north shore of Lake Superior in Minnesota. The 'cabin' we stayed in was beautifully situated in a remote area overlooking the lake about 20 miles from the Canadian border. After a pleasant afternoon gathering geological gems from the shores of Superior, we decided to open one of the treasures to admire the geode inside. An unsuccessful whack of the axe sent the rock leaping down the embankment to the bottom of the hill. Martha, one of our group, decided to retrieve the lost treasure and quickly began to sprint down part of the treacherously steep rocky terrain. Halfway down the hill she lost her footing, twisted to her left side as her head lead the way to the bottom just before the full length of her body collapsed onto the jumbled mass of rocks and boulders below. Those of us at the top of the hill could only scream in horror as we helplessly watched the scene unfold, silently wondering how to even get her to medical attention for the surely shattered bones.

No need. The Angels were surrounding and protecting Martha throughout the incredible journey. Her head never touched a jagged edge or unforgiving rock. Her arm and hand sustained scrapes as they found their way into a protective hole (or holy presence as we believe) as she landed. There were no sprains, strains, jammed fingers or broken bones. Martha was able to walk back up the hill by herself to her awaiting friends. We surrounded her with Healing Touch after we physically cleaned and attended to the scrapes. Martha awoke the next day feeling no stiffness or pain that should have accompanied such a body battering. She did receive the gift of a rainbow of colors on her arm during the healing process. We are all extremely thankful for the Angelic presence in Martha's miracle on September 4, 2006.

—Lovingly submitted by Mary Beth
Roswell, Georgia

Angels Warning

Glowing and White

My grandmother's name is Lily May Lovett. She was born in 1897 in Harlan County, Kentucky, pretty much in the hills. She told me this story when I was about 20 years old, which would have been about 1968.

Like so many people of her time, my grandmother lived near the railroad tracks when she was a small child. The kids she played with had been pushing a discarded flat-bed rail car up a small hill and then at the very top of the hill the kids would all jump on the car and ride it to the bottom to wherever it came to a halt. I guess the dangerous part was jumping onto the car, especially if you were my grandmother's age, which I remember to be about 5 or 6 at the time.

One day, according to my grandmother, an angel wearing a beautiful white gown and with a glow all around approached her and told her to keep away from the car as it was very dangerous. My grandmother told me she was the prettiest person she had ever seen.

When my grandmother told me the story she looked me straight in the eye and I could tell that she believed every word she was telling me. She often told me stories of the family and their times growing up in the hills of Kentucky. This one was different because there was no smile or twinkle in her eye to lead me to believe she was telling me anything but the honest to goodness truth.

The end result was that my grandmother did take the angel's advice and only watched the kids from a distance. That day a tragedy occurred and one of the kids was killed when they fell underneath the car as it was rolling down the hill.

—Bob Lovett
Marietta, Georgia

Highway Angels

During the late 1990's my son and I took many car trips to visit my daughter who moved from New Jersey to Georgia, as well as a yearly visit to my Mom in Florida. My son was in his late teens and was a new driver. He showed good driving skills and above all had a responsible attitude at the wheel so I felt comfortable letting him get some highway driving experience. On one of our trips to Florida, while he was driving, the entire front of the car lit up and was bathed in a beautiful purple light. I did not know what to make of it and I didn't want to startle him since it was clear that he wasn't seeing what I was. Within seconds our front tire blew and thank God that he kept command of the wheel and brought the car safely to the side of the road. I told him what I saw and as I guessed he had not seen anything. We were both a bit shaken and I was very grateful that he was able to handle the situation so well. I kept thinking about the light and wondering what it meant. A year or two later we were returning from a trip to Georgia and were reaching the approach to the New Jersey Turnpike. He was driving and I was pointing out to him that we needed to stay to the right to get onto the turnpike when once again I saw the purple light bathe the entire front of the car, inside and out. I was sure now that I knew what the light meant and even though I was expecting something to happen I tried to sound calm so as not to startle him. I told him to be alert and within seconds a driver going at least 80 mph realized that he wanted to get on the turnpike and he just turned his wheel right into our lane. Once again we managed to avoid a disastrous accident. After we both calmed down and realized how lucky we were I told him what I had

seen. Only now, I realized that we were being protected. I associate purple with the Angelic realm and
believe that the Angels were definitely looking out
for us. I have told anyone that travels with me in a
car what it means if I say "Purple Light."

—J.K. Sobel
amaham1@aol.com
Marietta, Georgia

Driving Instructions

My daughter was about three years old. For several
months I had been promising my husband that I
would check out a community center for a preschool
that we wanted to send our daughter to. I kept putting it off for some reason. That reason made itself
very clear to us later. Every time I thought about
going to that center, I just didn't feel right. I spoke
to my husband one day that I was prepared to take a
look at the place with our daughter the following
day. I told him I would go in the morning. As I drove
in the direction of the center, I started to feel hor-
rible...a sense of doom...I started to shake. The
closer to the center I got, the worse I felt.

I heard the words "drive in the other direction...don't go." I did exactly that. I turned my car
around and drove in the opposite direction. I felt

the urge to turn on the radio. Immediately I heard the newscaster talking about a shooting at the very center where I was supposed to be taking my daughter at the very time I would have been there. The man just came in and shot people for no reason whatsoever. Being that our daughter was not one to keep quiet, I feel the Angels saved her life in this instance. I think she would have said something to bring attention to herself and probably been shot.

—Hope Cramer, RMT, ATP®
Reiki, Spiritual Life Path Coach
reikihealingforu@aol.com, www.metaphysicalservices.com
Scottsdale, Arizona

Angels Appearing

My Vision

∽

The spiritual experience that changed my life was a visit from angels. Around 3 a.m. I was awakened from a deep sleep. I opened my eyes to see an amazing vision. On the right side of my body was a large angel! The angel appeared as a large orb of light which included all the colors of the spectrum. On either side of this orb, were large flapping white feathered wings. The angel flew above me and hovered for only a couple of seconds, before it disappeared and a clairvoyant picture show ran in my mind's eye. As if the movie was composed of black and white sketches, I saw a smiling angel flying above trees and nature. The angel appeared in a female form, but was a very crude sketch and the face appeared as a "happy face"—☺). I have read that angels can take any form and they often appear in the most unintimidating way possible, so that they do not frighten the viewer. The "picture show" was suddenly over and I looked up to magically see hundreds of these "happy face" angels staring down at me. This was a miracle to me. I had been visited by angels, and my life would never be the same. Angels are real!

—Cecily Channer, ATP, Divine Artistry
www.divineartistry.com
cecily@divineartistry.com
San Diego, California

Archangel Michael

Angels have always been a part of my life. I always believed in a higher source, and felt safe and protected on my journey. A spiritual seeker for more than half my life, the experience of healing from breast cancer propelled me forward. I began to realize my potential as a healer, first for myself, and then others.

My learning process and dissatisfaction with allopathic medicine to heal the "whole" me urged me to investigate alternative healing. Reiki called out to me through articles and conversation. My body and energy responded and within 6 months I completed my training as a Reiki Master, able to pass this loving energy on, and to teach others. Thus, I began my journey into various healing modalities (EMF Balancing Technique, Spiritual Response Therapy, Angel Therapy, Chrystalline Consciousness Technique, and ARCHES Healing). Each step firmed my connection with and my ability to see, hear, feel and know Divine Guidance.

Of the angelic kingdom, the being that I work with the most, on a daily basis actually, is Archangel Michael. I remember years ago the first time I connected with his essence. I had received a message in meditation that a new guide would be coming through to me. I prepared myself to receive this gift with intention and entered a meditative state asking to meet him/her.

I sat outside surrounded by nature, and surrendered into an altered state. I realized a presence in front of me. "Boy are you tall," I exclaimed as I looked up and up. A cobalt blue light reached up to a height of at least 20 feet. Feelings of love, safety, security flooded through me. Tears streamed down my face, and I felt overwhelmed, even a little unworthy to be in such a presence.

"Please relax. I am here to offer you support. Feel free to call upon me at any time. I am always here for you. I'll help you cut away any negativity that you might encounter. Nothing stands in your way. Be the healer that you are. I'd love for you to be a part of my Band of Mercy, the many lightworkers that share the light to the world."

Needless to say, this experience greatly
enhanced my confidence and courage. I knew that
I was on the right path. I ask Michael to be with me
in every session that I do for myself or others. I began
to see him with more human features: tall, handsome, blond, strong, almost always carrying a sword.

Michael offered me my very own sword during
another time we shared. The handle filled with
purple and red precious stones leads to a long, silver, shiny saber. I use it to keep light around me,
and strengthen my boundaries. Michael has also
offered some of my clients their own sword, the
most amazing was an eight year old who had been
abandoned by her mother.

During my Angel Therapy training with Dr.
Doreen Virtue, Michael came through her leading
the group of 150 on a powerful meditation that
filled each of us with so much light and energy we
felt it for days afterward.

Angels enrich my life. They help me to fulfill
my greatest potential by leading me to the experiences that most benefit me. I ask them for all kinds
of things from parking spaces to computer help to
finding the best book—the list is endless. One time
my husband had been having trouble with his
motor cycle. In fact, he'd been trying to fix it for
over a week. I finally asked for the mechanic angels

to help him solve the problem. And within 15 minutes he had it started and took off for a ride.

I live in gratitude every minute for the blessings
they bring into my life.

—LeeAnn Wehr CRM, ATP
angelhelp4u@msn.com
Tucson, Arizona

Angels Reassuring

I was 31 years old and had suffered three miscarriages. The last one was particularly traumatic since I was four months pregnant and an ultrasound failed to show any movement. A specialist was called in to confirm the ultrasound and I knew something was wrong, but the doctor would not tell me anything until my own doctor talked to me. I did not miscarry but had to wait two weeks to be scheduled for a D & C. It was emotionally painful and those around me could not offer me comfort. About a month afterwards my brother and his wife had a baby girl. I went to the hospital and was looking through the viewing window to see her. I was standing a little back from my husband and my sister-in-law. I was looking at the baby and I had the sensation of a hand being laid gently on my right shoulder and the sensation of a voice saying that it was all right now. There was nothing to be afraid of. Everything will be fine. I became pregnant within ten days and delivered my first son.

—Cindy Snowball
Bradenton, Florida

Angel Feathers

This is a small story, but one that I cherish. I am a breast cancer survivor and, looking back, I believe now that this adventure is one of the best life gifts I have received. However, at the time it was painful. I was constantly fatigued, always living with constant nausea, feeling ugly most of the time. But I will say that I have never felt that God does not love me. I have felt God's hands on me and there is no feeling with which to compare.

One day after a chemo session I had returned home and was lying on my couch wondering if my stomach would lose control any second. I've always off-set the feeling of nausea by being still, very still. I felt so sad and started to cry softly. My mom, a flesh and blood angel was in the other room and I did not want her to worry so I sobbed only to myself. And I talked to God saying, "Father, if this disease is going to kill me, please let it take me now. I'm tired and it is so difficult to fight every day and still try to keep a positive attitude. I need to know if there is hope for me." Instantly the room was filled with the most beautiful shimmering tiny feathers. Some folks might say I was delirious, but I know these were angel feathers sent by God to brighten my path. I knew then and never once again doubted that I would be okay, healthy and happy.

—Dianah Foster
Butterflygirl7@adelphia.net
Cartersville, Georgia

Angels to the Rescue

I had stopped to help a person with an ailing car on the side of the road since I knew a lot about fixing cars. As I was working on the man's car, without warning he cranked the motor, resulting in an instant explosion. My face, head and shoulders were ablaze and I dashed for a creek I had seen as I approached the stricken car, the flames searing my body. I went into the creek head first, dousing the flames quickly.

I felt nothing. My legs and feet had come up over my shoulders but I couldn't feel them. I was in great physical shape since I ran and did weight training regularly at 28 years old, but now my stomach muscles had no strength. My breathing became shallow and difficult and I wondered if I was leaving this planet. I saw the man who I was helping standing at the top of the embankment and told him to go for help. I knew he couldn't hear me because no sound came from my lips, but perhaps he would know to go for help. I thought of my wife and family and hoped they'd be okay. I had no control over my body; I couldn't get up.

As I floated in that creek I suddenly felt as if I was being embraced. A feeling of great love engulfed me and I became very peaceful. I heard a voice inside of me say that I was about to learn more about myself than I had ever dreamed. A surge of excitement pulsed through me and I thought how crazy this was, that it was nuts to be feeling this given my present situation.

I beat the odds and lived but a wheel chair became my legs. It was devastating and from that moment on my life changed dramatically. I know that God and the angels were with me at the moment I needed them to help me understand that there was a reason for it all beyond what I knew. The spiritual experience in the creek was profound and of prime importance in my healing process. God and the angels were there for me when I needed them the most and have remained with me daily as I recreated my life.

—Harry O'Brien
Atlanta Recording Studio
hobrienjr@comcast.net
Kennesaw, Georgia

Angel Wings

Many years ago I was purchasing my first home. I had applied for a mortgage but was concerned about my application being accepted because the mortgage broker had told me: "with your income, you couldn't buy a bicycle".

One late afternoon, I was sitting in my office at work fretting over this situation. I had my eyes closed, silently strategizing about what I would do if I didn't get to move into my new home. All of a sudden, I sensed what felt to be two enormously large and kind "wings" gently enfolding me — it was like a warm and soothing presence was putting his arms around me! At the same time, I heard a silent message with clear words telling me that "I was not to worry because everything would be taken care of."

Needless to say, I got the mortgage without a hitch! Years later I realized it had been Archangel Michael who had assisted me. The day it happened I knew little about Angels—only what I had learned in church!

—Dawn Dhyanna, ATP
dhyannai@comcast.net
Healdsburg, California

Angels Guiding

Angel Sign

〰

I never had a near-death experience or anything that dramatic prior to becoming an Angel Therapy Practitioner. I was already certified in Reiki and just knew it was the next step to helping my clients receive guidance from other realms. I bought one of Doreen Virtue's Angel card decks and, voila, I was hooked on Angel Readings. I had been staying at home with my son and knew I didn't want to go back to teaching middle school French.

I had a nagging feeling to go to training with Doreen in April of 2006. I asked Archangel Ariel to give me a sign (I had formed a bond with her in my own healing the few months prior) to know if I should go to California, as I would have to leave my 16 month-old son at home for five days. In the next instant after I asked Ariel the question, I turned on the television to the Travel Channel and they were featuring a hotel, not just any hotel, but the Monarch St. Regis where the training was going to be held. I took this as a clear sign that I should go. The Angels teach us to "Be awake to our good!"

I am ever so grateful for that message, the training itself, and the healing it entailed for me and the other participants, which was life-altering. If you're ready for your life to change, start invoking your Angels to help guide you. If you're willing to go with the flow, things will begin to change very quickly.

—Andrea R. Wagner, ATP and Reiki Practitioner
www.AngelPeace.com
Albany, New York

Heavenly Decor

About 4 years ago, my husband and I were decorating our new home and decided to add decor that emphasized our spiritual background. We were still in the throes of "born again" passion that I had heard so much about from other new Christians.

I found an awesome portrait of Jesus as "The Rabbi" teacher that He was, and some other splendid items but, somehow we just weren't satisfied with our efforts. One day I envisioned a cross that should be placed in the foyer above the front door. My husband said that it would be difficult to find a cross that would be exactly what I wanted. He offered to make it himself.

I knew he had some expertise working with wood, but I was a bit skeptical about his ability to complete the cross exactly as I envisioned it. In any case, we agreed that I should go to the home improvement store and look for the appropriate materials. I didn't know exactly why, but I felt very strongly that there should be no nails or screws or glue. Only natural materials could be used in making this project.

As I walked into the store, I explained my project to the clerk and he promptly told me where the wood was located. I found the aisle and remembered thinking that it was a good time of day to shop as there were not many customers around, especially in this area. I began looking through the small pile of boards that looked like long 2 inch square staffs. I rejected several before I found two that caught my eye. I held them both up in front of me to inspect them so I could make a selection.

I was startled as I felt something or someone right next to me! I turned slightly and saw that it was a very handsome "older" gentleman with a most serene demeanor, including eyes that seemed to sparkle and reflect sunlight. (Indoors?) "The one on the right, my dear, it's perfect," he said in a low but commanding voice. "Do not use nails, screws, glue, lacquer, or any unnatural materials." "Anoint your finished product with olive oil."

I was amazed that he knew what I had planned. I turned to glance at the wood and instantly back to him. Once again I was startled as the stranger was no longer there! I didn't see him or anyone else walking down the aisle in either direction. I quickly returned the unwanted board to its temporary home and hurried to the register with my treasure. I was glad that I didn't have to wait at the register.

While driving home, I tried to understand what happened at the store. Was it real or just hysteria because of my new found passion? Later that day, I showed the wood to my husband and told him about using only natural resources to complete the cross. He knew exactly what to do, and a couple hours later, he came in from the work shop with the finished cross in hand. He had carved out the wood so that both pieces crossed exactly together. I couldn't figure out how he accomplished this!

We mounted it in place above the front door and the whole foyer seemed to brighten! This time I wasn't the only one having an "epiphany." Standing next to me, my husband beamed with joy with tears in his eyes because he was able to complete the project as ordered.

We praised God for giving us the construction plans and thanked Him for sending us his best foreman. I think I know what that whirring sound was when I looked for him down the aisle.

Don't large wings make a similar sound when flapping?

—Mary Harder, Executive Producer
Glorybridge Productions
www.Glorybridgeproductions.com
San Antonio, Texas

How Could You Possibly Know That?

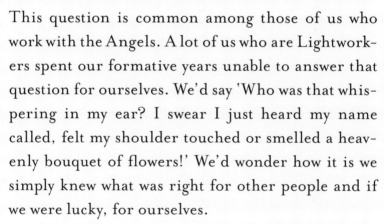

This question is common among those of us who work with the Angels. A lot of us who are Lightworkers spent our formative years unable to answer that question for ourselves. We'd say 'Who was that whispering in my ear? I swear I just heard my name called, felt my shoulder touched or smelled a heavenly bouquet of flowers!' We'd wonder how it is we simply knew what was right for other people and if we were lucky, for ourselves.

I did not take a direct path to the Angels. I meandered through the 8-year, 3-school college plan, had the Art Career, built a great marriage, had a gorgeous baby and finally ended up still happily discontented before I realized the calling of the Angels was there all along. Before then I was unable to understand that the "coincidences" in my life were in fact not coincidences at all, the 'knowing' I had experienced was Divine Guidance and the free counseling I gave people in my life was worth building a career on.

After I read all the books on Lightworkers, Angels, and Mediumship that I could get my hands on, I realized that working for the Angels is perfect for me. After meditation, training and practice I found the Angel and Spirits were waiting for me to get started. I had clients before my business was even begun and began to feel in loving harmony with my Divine Life Purpose. In the beginning, before each session, my ego would rise and tell me I was making it all up, that I must be a great story teller, that I was merely quick on my feet and good with advice. But each session has without fail allowed me to hear specific messages for the client that I couldn't possibly have dreamed up, messages of healing and joy that each client needed at that very moment. Messages were given to me through their words, pictures and thoughts that I would easily interpret for the person seeking their advice. I used to be somewhat stunned every time the Angels and Archangels came through so clearly and I would be in tears at the power of their lovely bright presence! I would even be surprised when the client responded with joy and excitement to the reading, wondering if it could possibly be as profound for them as it was for me. I used to mentally say "Whew!" in relief that I was on target. But then I realized something of the utmost importance to those of us who work with Angels; we are doing very little in these sessions! We are simply opening ourselves to their messages and it is not us 'performing' at all! That took a load of fear away from my practice and my self-awareness. I am free, knowing that the Angels work through me for the highest good of my clients and myself.

The experience of being chosen to work with the Angels has done so much for me and my life. My self-esteem has healthfully skyrocketed, my faith in people has increased immeasurably, and my relationship with the Angels has become the biggest and most important bond in my existence. The Angels are waiting to speak to each and every one of us and if you sit still silently you will be able to hear them too! How could I possibly know that? Because my Angels said so!

—Janis McKay Babcock, ATP
Spirited Angel
www.SpiritedAngel.com
St Paul, Minnesota

Angelic Presence

I've always felt an angelic presence, even as a child. Yet, the most concrete proof of their existence happened in my adult life when my mother returned as an angel and helped an instantaneously healing for me from twenty-seven years of excruciating back pain. Now, I work and play with angels daily. They help me in activities from the most mundane to the most extraordinary.

A crowded parking lot with no spaces available? I ask my angels for help and soon a car pulls out, welcoming me into its slot.

I'm stuck in a major traffic tie-up for nearly an hour. A ribbon of cars lay ahead. Fellow motorists who had trekked ahead to the scene of the accident reported back that police officials expected another two hours of delay. I called upon my angels to get the traffic moving. Fifteen minutes later the highway shoulder is opened to allow cars to roll.

My intuition told me to call in my angels for help while boarding a flight in Alaska. I discovered a gray energy inside passengers as they boarded. We banked sharply forty-five minutes into the flight. The pilot informed us that we had smoke in the cockpit and are returning to the airport. I'm an uneasy flyer in the best of circumstances. Yet, I remained calm and peaceful throughout our return.

Angels are ready and willing to help all of us. All we need to do is ask. Their assistance has given me a feeling of power that comes from knowing that I am not alone. I am connected to my God-source through them. My angels have brought more joy to my life and given me an appreciation of the magic that life provides.

—Marilyn Segal, ATP
Workshops, Life Purpose Readings
www.TwinWisdom.com
Atlanta, Georgia and Boca Raton, Florida

Angels are Here to Help Us

I've had many instances of Angels and beings from the other side throughout my life. Here though, I wish to talk about Angels, since they have helped to guide me so much and helped get me out of trouble so many times. Interestingly enough, one instance has to do with why I'm conversing with you right now; the Angels got a message across to me about writing. Several years back after I received one of my Reiki attunements, I was experiencing some interesting phenomena. One that stands out in my mind was how my Angels reminded me through a message that I had put aside my love of writing for other pursuits in my life.

One day I received an e-mail out of the blue from some stranger. It had something to do with a writing course. I thought, "That's interesting, but I really don't have time for that," so I ignored it. *Delete* Then a day or two later, a new client mentioned she thought that she and I would make a great team for writing a book on Angels. I thought "Interesting," but nothing every really came of it. The second message was more clear and specific than the first one. I said to my Angels "Okay, if this is supposed to be a message, then I'll only believe it if I get it a third time, and make it something I can't miss!" I had a prove-it-to-me attitude at the time.

The next morning, I woke up and went into the kitchen, preparing to get my daughter her breakfast before school. There on the kitchen floor was my tennis shoe, just sitting in the middle of the floor. I thought, "Okay, this is odd. I know I didn't leave a shoe in the kitchen last night. I went to bed after my husband and my daughter and it wasn't there when I went to sleep." My daughter wasn't awake yet, but I called my husband at his work. I asked him "Honey, did you somehow accidentally kick one of my tennis shoes into the kitchen?" He said "No, it wasn't there when I left for work." After a few moments he asked me "Hope, which shoe is it, the left or the right shoe?"

I took the phone into the kitchen and looked. It was the right shoe. He said "there's your third message!" Write, write and right!!! Clear as day. From then on, I usually did not require my Angels to work quite so hard to get messages through to me. I thought if they can take the time and energy to physically manifest a message like that, I should at least take the time to listen!

—Hope Cramer, RMT, ATP®
Reiki, Spiritual Life Path Coach
reikihealingforu@aol.com, www.metaphysicalservices.com
Scottsdale, Arizona

Angels Healing

Tumor Healed

For a couple years I had been calling upon my Angels for comfort and healing. In 2000, I developed a large, painful tumor on the inside of my right breast which my doctor thought was cancer. Fibrocystic breasts had plagued me most of my life. This tumor happened just prior to my menses and it literally grew overnight. It was very large, about the size of a golf ball. Of course, I believed that it would disappear the same way it appeared. However, that was not to be.

On the second night, I was awakened by excruciating pain in my right breast. It was about three o'clock in the morning. I got up and looked for a pain killer. I don't keep those around because I do not take drugs. So I took some aspirin, drank some water and decided to go back to bed and try to sleep. I lay down and put both my hands over the tumor and prayed to my Angels. "Please Angels, take the pain away and let me sleep, let me sleep, let me sleep, let me sleep." That was the mantra I repeated until I fell asleep. The next morning, I awoke in the same position, and was surprised that my pain was much less.

After about three days, I decided to go to my doctor because it was not going away as I had hoped. My doctor was very upset with me and, because he had already had breast cancer, he considered this the same thing. As much as I loved this doctor, he really put fear into me. I can still see him sitting at his desk just shaking his head back and forth. He had the phone in his hand to call his oncologist for me. I was not convinced, so feeling very scared and nervous, I told him I had to sleep on it. His genuine and concerned comment was, "Don't wait too long, because you only get one chance and you could die." He knew I was a Holistic Health Practitioner and commented that my "holistic" ways were good for colds but not for this.

After much soul-searching and meditating, I decided not to go to the oncologist but do my own thing. That consisted of following my intuition and angel guidance to do healing visualizations three times a day. I called on Michael (the Archangel) to assist me in using a psychic vacuum to take out all the darkness from my whole body starting at my head down to my toes. Then I'd focus and "imagine" the tumor gone. This was the tough part, because the tumor was there, so how can one imagine it not there? I gave myself four months (until Christmas) for it to be healed. I'm delighted to say that the tumor was gone well before Thanksgiving! Thank you God and Angels.

—Ann Lisette Wesso
Author, Certified Spiritual Counselor
www.annwesso.com
Reno, Nevada

Relationship Healed

I turned fifty years young last year. I felt like changes were in store for me and in many ways I was ready. I had been estranged from my son (Josh) for almost a year and I wanted that to change more than anything! The last time we had spoken on the phone, I had screamed at him. I can't remember ever being so angry. I felt like he had been disrespectful and I had done nothing to deserve it.

I was at the end of my rope in the situation but didn't know what to do. I had gone to therapy and read several self-help books. Doreen Virtue's "Healing with Angels" book had a profound effect on me and I was using techniques that she described. One day I prayed to Archangel Michael to please help me. He gave me the message that "there is nothing on the earthbound plane that you can do to heal Josh. If you want to find peace in your heart for this situation, you must try to look at Josh through his angels' eyes."

This really made sense to me. I knew that we all had guardian angels and that they only came from a place of love. If I could heal myself with my angels, then maybe the same could also work to heal this situation. I was desperate and open to anything. I started this and immediately felt something different. I felt like some toxic emotions were melting away.

A few weeks later, I found myself in a situation of unexpectedly counseling a friend about his relationship with his father. I used the angel technique that Michael had given me on him not knowing if he could relate. As I drove away from his house, I said to myself "you can't do the talk unless you do the walk." I picked up my cell phone and called my son Josh without the fear that had stopped me so many times before. I was disappointed when he didn't answer, but he called me back immediately. We talked for a while about nothing in particular but I felt good about making the call.

Josh is thirty-one and I had this ominous feeling that if I hadn't called him, he might not ever call me again. A few weeks later, I called him again and this time he said he was coming down to Austin to visit. Josh had never come to see me without an agenda, so it made me curious, but I didn't care. It seemed like a miracle to me.

My wife and I were a little apprehensive about the visit after all that had happened, but that all disappeared when we saw him. We hugged like nothing had happened in the past. We went to the park and played Frisbee with several friends like we had done in the past every Wednesday for several years. Some of them that knew our story were a little shocked to see him there. We played and laughed like children. He later said he had timed it that way intentionally.

It was the weekend before his birthday and we watched movies and really enjoyed ourselves. He didn't seem to have any agenda and it was fine with me to keep things light and upbeat. I saw a softness in his eyes for this was an answered prayer. What I had considered a complex problem now seemed simple. Before he left I told him my anger was for the disrespect he had shown me. He tried to explain to me in his own way why he acted this way before he left.

After dinner we sent him on his way. My wife and I talked about it all the way home. I felt a large burden had been lifted from my shoulders as we returned home. We walked in the door and saw something that was nothing short of angelic. We had a Christmas Cactus that was a wedding gift. It was thirty years old and the oldest living thing we cared for in our home. We knew this plant very well. It only bloomed at Christmas and for several years never bloomed at all. The last few years it was prolific at Christmas with several blooms. When it did bloom it was always the entire plant. We couldn't believe our eyes. It had a single bloom on the plant and it was March. It takes a cold snap to evoke blooms and Texas in March is not in any way cold.

I searched the plant for any other buds but found none. We took it as a sign from Jesus and the angels that a real healing had occurred. It was white which to me signified love. We were so taken with this that Beckie and I both took pictures of it and stored them in my computer.

Josh and I are talking regularly now and rebuilding our relationship at a good pace. I am finding peace in my heart even as I know we still have a ways to go, but that I now have tools to help me.

I was getting ready for my trip to California for a certification with Doreen Virtue as an Angel Therapist® and decided to print a photo to tape on the cover of my journal. Now mind you, I have printed several pictures over the years without any abnormalities. I nearly fell over when this picture came out with this beautiful bloom. It is a white flower with green stems and a brown wall background. The photo shows the white bloom totally engulfed in purple! This is the color of Archangel Michael's aura. I took it as his way of affirmation. Thank you Michael!

Note: As I wrote this story my scrollbar never went to the bottom. I hit it twice accidentally and below this writing were two words. Wow! For me there is no doubt! I left those two words at the bottom for all to see.

angels, maybe

—Russell Forsyth, ATP
russellforsyth@sbcglobal.net
Austin, TX

Amazing Earth Angels

About 7 years ago, I was diagnosed with melanoma cancer. I had gone for a routine check-up at my Naturopath (ND). It was mostly for internal digestive problems due to stress. For some wild reason, my ND asked to look at my leg. She kept on focusing on it, then called the head ND and asked for her opinion. They both agreed that my skin looked marbled. I thought it was a nice chat between two ND's who had fun making a diagnosis on a young mid-thirties busy patient. I couldn't wait to get out of the office; after all I was there for my headaches and stomachaches. I was a busy lady, working for GE at the time.

I got home, and at the time was living with a guy that had lost his wife to melanoma a few years back. I asked him about my marbled leg and showed him an unusual mole and his face went grey. He got on the phone and made an appointment with a dermatologist. Needless to stay, I got the appointment fairly quickly and two weeks later received a message to call the dermatologist immediately. On Monday I received the news that it was cancer and was immediately scheduled for surgery the next week to remove the cancer by a plastic surgeon. Wow, talk about having my angels lined up and making things happen for me so quickly. Fast forward, a few months later, the surgery was completed, but I felt terribly empty and shallow. My life at GE wasn't the same anymore. Life had a new meaning; I didn't understand any of my friends. My colleagues and my job didn't make sense anymore. I saw my MD and she said: "You are having anxiety attacks and I have a new treatment for you." Boy, the meds she gave me threw me off balance, made me go green. Well, she had more goodies for me—another pill for depression which made me feel worse, and the side effects—20 pounds heavier in 3 weeks! Lovely new portrait of me, making me feel more lost and restless. Now I was a former shadow of myself. A dear friend called me out of the blue and said, "Nat, you're not yourself, you sound depressed. What's up?" Now Wendy, my friend, is a logical, rational thinker who doesn't buy the angel bit! What a hoot that was! I felt like the Supreme Being (God) had sent his best messenger through Wendy's mouth, as the pills and the reactions of my body weren't loud and clear enough for me to get the message! It took someone like her, who had never said anything like this to me before, to wake me up. I was stunned and decided to really listen to the message, not the messenger. It was simply in me and I had decided that if Wendy, the Doubting Thomas could speak like that, I had to wake up for good and see the mess I had made by feeling sorry for myself! Ouch!

From there, my life went into a spin cycle. Shortly thereafter I gave my notice at GE, walked away from three years of hard work and went looking for the new chapter and meaning in my life. Unlike Buddha, I didn't have time to sit under a tree for 20 years. Instead, I signed up for a Certification in Hypnotherapy, took two years to complete a Coach U degree (became a Life Coach), and through this proceeded to complete the ATP class with Doreen Virtue. It's throughout this drama that I made a few best friends for life, took four years of sabbatical when I was young and alive and redirected my life. How many angels do you count in this story? I'll tell you there are angels in most of the people that I've met during my healing. If you're simply willing to open your eyes, especially the third eye, you'll see them everywhere around you. From the naturopath to the dermatologist, the plastic surgeon, the RN's at all the offices I visited who greeted me like a human, not a sick patient, and to the friends who looked at me with envy when I told them I was done with my empty life. So many of them were angels in their own way; they all assisted in getting me back on my path.

—Natali Wall, ATP
Spiritual Coach Indigo Blue Angels
www.indigoblueangels.com
Norwich, Connecticut

Angels Comforting

Birds and Angels Fly

My dad had transitioned to the other side and I missed him, so I asked God and the angels to help me connect with him. I began to see birds everywhere, lots of birds. My dad had always loved and enjoyed birds. But it was getting freaky that so many birds seemed to be near me everywhere I went.

One day I went for an early morning walk by myself and noticed lots of birds flying around me, and many of them were red. I was wondering if maybe my dad was talking to me through the birds, so I asked in my mind "Dad, is this a message from you?" Immediately a bright red bird flew up out of the tall grass near my feet as I was walking. It landed on the ground near my foot and began hopping all around, giving the appearance of dancing. It continued to do this while I walked, staying close to me. Suddenly it flew into the air beside me and followed along side me in a straight line as I walked. Something was surely going on here so I asked in my mind "Is that you dad? Are you trying to get my attention?" I heard a voice inside of me say "You're on track. Just keep right on going." A feeling of peace flooded me and I felt so happy that he and I had connected. This red bird continued flying in a straight line beside me as I walked. When I finished my walk I said "Goodbye dad." And the red bird flew away. To me the most amazing part of this story is the fact that the bird seemed to be waiting for me and flew out of the grass just as I asked if this was my dad connecting to me. It truly was an experience I'll always treasure.

—Annie Pinto
Angel Practitioner
anniekay33@yahoo.com
Marietta, Georgia

The Angel of Death: The Most Tender Angel

My angel story begins in 1982, during the funeral of a cousin who died under mysterious circumstances. At the time all our family knew was that Marjorie's body had been found drowned in a pond near her home. She could not swim and speculation by law enforcement authorities was that she either drowned accidentally, committed suicide, or was murdered. Our family believed there was foul play because no one who knew her thought her capable of committing suicide. But who would want to murder her? She was always the one telling funny jokes and stories, and wherever she was there was laughter.

By the time Marjorie's death occurred, I had been aware of my extended sense perceptions of clairaudience and clairvoyance for about ten years, and I wondered if, at her funeral, I might perceive something. As I sat during the service, I was astonished to see a huge angel suspended in mid-air above her casket. Since my family is made up of conservative Methodists, I knew I could not point to the angel and yell, "Do y'all see that?" Instead, I watched, and hoped I could get a clue as to whether or not she had been murdered. As I attuned myself to Marjorie during the service, I heard hysterical crying and her voice screaming, "I shouldn't have done it! I shouldn't have done it!" For many years I wondered what really happened. If she was murdered, why would she be saying that?

A few years passed and I moved with my husband to Northern Virginia to live and work in 1983. My husband passed away in 1985 and after floundering for a period of time, I found myself in a new career teaching software classes at a federal law enforcement agency in Washington, D.C.

Near Christmas of 1990 a co-worker gave me the book entitled *Angels: An Endangered Species* by

Malcolm Godwin. As I flipped through the pages of the rather voluminous book, I was amazed to find that, on page 165, there was a picture of the angel I had seen at Marjorie's funeral. No credits were given in the book for the origin of the picture: an angel suspended in mid-air above a body of water. But it was an exact rendition of the one I remembered, except for the water.

The students in the class I was teaching that week were very open to the same subjects I had been involved in for so long: meditation, intuition, near death experiences. During breaks, we had some interesting discussions. One of the students in that class was a man in his late thirties named Joseph. I had already noticed his quietness, his serenity, and thought him rather unusual when I compared his demeanor to that of other students I had in the class.

I had a conversation with Joseph that week which revealed why he stood out from the others. A few years before, he said, he was driving home after work when a bus hit his car. He was critically injured in the accident and rushed to the nearest emergency room. As emergency personnel tried to save his life, he found himself outside his body, in the midst of a near death experience. He told me that an angel came to him and asked if he wanted to go on to the Other Side of life, or stay. Joseph chose to stay and there followed many months of recovery. I asked him how the near death experience had changed him, and his reply was, "I go to church now and spend more time with my family."

Next day I took the Angel book to class. During break I showed it to Joseph, slowly flipping the pages, watching to see if he reacted. At page 165, he exclaimed, "That¹s it! That looks just like the angel I saw when I almost died!" We had seen the same angel in our separate experiences.

So, was it the Angel of Death? I think so. This angel is known as the most tender angel of all. One only had to watch a few episodes of "Touched By An Angel" to get a sense of its wonderful compassion. As for my cousin Marjorie, about fourteen years after her death, I spoke with two of her surviving brothers and asked them if there had ever been an official ruling on the cause of her death. Both said that the day Marjorie died, she returned home from running errands, removed her jewelry and watch, told her husband she was going back into the small town where she lived, and, instead, drove to a nearby pond and drowned herself. Although most members of our family were unaware of it, she had been very depressed, and her death was ruled a suicide.

I have read many accounts of messages received from suicides after their death, expressing deep regret for having ended their life, and, for me, that explained her hysteria on the day of her funeral. It is my hope that Marjorie is now at peace.

—Rev. Patricia Warden
Spiritual & Intuitive Counseling, Numerology
wardenmp@earthlink.net
Gainesville, Georgia

Melinda

As an Angel Therapy Practitioner, I work with angels constantly. And from my first conscious memory as a child, I have always talked with angels. I have had so many experiences of being helped and loved by angels. I cannot imagine not relying on angels!

One experience with angels really stood out, though. I was in a session with a client from Houston, Texas whose young adult daughter had been killed in an auto accident right before Christmas. It seemed to be such a tragic loss of life. However, when I asked the angels for a message about this young woman whose name is Melinda, the angels showed me a very happy young woman.

Melinda sent a message through the angels showing her work with others weaving a cloth over the entire world. They showed me that when we are kind to others, the cloth is woven. When we are fearful, angry or resentful, there is a hole. They explained that this is a cloth of healing, love and peace. Melinda and others are working above and we are needed to work here on the earth.

As the angels showed me how this cloth is woven, they told me that when we act out of kindness and love, we are helping to bring love and peace to the earth. When you allow another car into traffic ahead of you, when you respond with kindness to a family member who has irritated you, when you treat yourself with love and kindness, you are doing your part to weave this cloth of love and peace. When you complain or feel angry or worry, you are leaving a hole.

Angels have told me many times that they are here to help with anything we need. Life is not meant to be a struggle, they say. They say everyone's most important purpose is to be kind and to love ourselves and others.

—Margaret Staton, MA, ATP
Spiritual Counselor and Life Coach
healingangel334@hotmail.com, www.angelscommunicator.com
Orlando, Florida

Angels Come When You Need It Most

In my life, I have experienced several different signs that proved to me that my Guardian Angel or angels were watching over me. Never did that prove to be more true then a couple of years ago.

In July of 2003, my husband and I were devastated when we got a phone call one Sunday morning that my husband's brother and sister-in-law were both tragically killed in a car accident in Texas. We lived outside of Atlanta, GA and immediately prepared to make the long drive to Texas so we could help decide on funeral arrangements as well as grieve with all of our family.

We knew that after the conversation with our sister-in-law months earlier it was the wish of our loved ones that they be cremated. Neither one had ever put together a will. My mother-in-law wanted to say her goodbyes, so my husband and I made arrangements with the funeral director and we drove her to the funeral home to view them. Before we left, we asked if any of my sister-in-law's family wanted to go along. In their sorrow, they declined. I had a close friendship with my sister-in-law and at one time we had worked together, so I felt that if no one else was able to be there for her, I would be.

My mother-in-law wept and it was very hard to watch her pain, but I have always had a strong faith so I knew in my heart that my brother-in-law and sister-in-law were at peace. Upon our departure from the funeral home, I walked up to the box that held my sister-in-law, tapped it three times and told her I would see her later, when it was my time to depart from this world. It was a very sad day but I felt better for being able to say my goodbyes.

The next morning, I woke up, but was still lying in the bed when I felt three strong taps on my shoulder. I turned to see if my husband had done it, but he was sound asleep and several feet away from me on the other side of a king size bed. It took a minute for me as I tried to figure out who tapped me on the shoulder, but then I had a feeling of comfort come over me as I realized that my sister-in-law was trying to tell me that she was okay and had seen me at the funeral home the day before. I shared my experience with the rest of my family later that morning.

I know that angels are watching over us with anticipation when we reunite someday. There are times when I see someone who reminds me of my sister-in-law, and I miss her but I feel so privileged that she chose to come to me and let me know she was okay during that sorrowful time. I learned that we must never overlook the signs our loved ones send us to let us know that they still love us and that they are okay. What a blessing.

—Karen S. Parker
kspflem@aol.com
Acworth, Georgia

Angels Assisting

The Mysterious Stranger

I was moving from my friend's house to my present home back in July of 1999. I had rented a U-haul and had stopped to put gas in it. I tried to pull the large U-haul around the pump but instead I wrapped it around the pump. I was stuck. I became very upset and thought I was going to have to purchase a new pump for the gas station. I could not get anyone to come help me when all of a sudden this woman, a stranger, walked up to me and said "I will help you." She got into the U-haul and proceeded to back it up. When I looked everything seemed pretty much okay. I told her I'd be right back and I went into the station to speak with the attendant. However, when I turned around the woman had disappeared. I never got to tell her thank you. I was certainly relieved when she appeared to help me. The gas station did not charge me for any damages and told me not to worry about anything, that all was fine. I went on my way but was quite badly shaken over all that had happened. It was as if God sent her to me! I know she was an angel.

—Maggie Steck
Real Estate Agent
Roswell, Georgia

Angels Open the Door

Angels have played an important part in my life in some profound, deep, and intense circumstances, but I also know that they can be helpful in very simple, everyday, and commonplace situations.

Several years ago, I attended a business retreat with a number of coworkers in a location several hours from our office. The men planned to stay in one location (a private home owned by our CEO), and the women in another (a home that had been rented for us for the weekend). A terrible rain storm with thunder and lightning had knocked out power in the town to which we were heading, so we were required to drive to a town even further away, and had to find a temporary location that could accommodate the beginning of our retreat. By late afternoon, we were all very tired, very hot, very sticky, very hungry, and as the result, very irritable. Finally, we were able to head to our original destination, the women stopping to retrieve the key to our weekend home. The original women's rental home was no longer available due to the weather, so our office manager received a key to a different rental home, and we headed to it. When we arrived, the keys we'd been given did not seem to fit any of the locks to any of the doors. The office manager tried all the keys in all the locks, as did several other of my female coworkers. They jiggled, removed, and replaced the keys in the various locks, and nothing worked. Finally, I asked for the keys. Before I placed the first key in the first lock, I asked my angels to do whatever they needed to do to help us get in. With absolutely no difficulty, the first key I'd chosen went into the lock, the lock turned, and the door opened.

—Dawna E. Wade, ATP
www.AngelGuided.com
Dawna@AngelGuided.com
Black Mountain, North Carolina

Angels Find the Way

In addition to doing angel readings, I am also an insurance investigator and work on the road driving to locations to meet people. On one such occasion, I was driving in an unfamiliar location and had been driving in circles for awhile, looking for a particular street. I simply could not find it and I was getting very late for the appointment. Finally (I don't know why it took me so long) I said, "Okay, Angels, you need to get me there!" As I turned down a street to make a u-turn there was a car stopped at the top of the street and a man was frantically waving his arm out of the window at me. I was a bit concerned, but rolled down my window anyway and looked at him quizzically. He said, "Are you lost?" I was shocked and confused that this total stranger was asking me this question. I laughed and said, "Actually, I am." He asked me what street I was looking for and then pointed to the top of his car and said, "I'm pizza delivery, I know every street around here." I just couldn't believe what I was hearing. Seeing the pizza delivery sign on the top of his car, made me feel better about telling this man where I needed to go. I told him and he said, "Follow me, I'll take you right there."

Sure enough, he drove me right to the person's door! He didn't stick around for any thank you, but just drove away! I have chills as I write this because I know without a doubt that the Angels stepped right in and took care of me in the very instant that I asked. There have been so many other times the Angels have helped me, countless times, and they will help anyone who asks. The key to having angelic help is simply to ask!

—Lisa A. Grilo ATP®
Angel Bridge
angelbridgelisa@hotmail.com
Plymouth, Maine

Angels by My Side

One time that I knew I was definitely not alone was during the trial for my sexual assault. I was about to start the fourth grade in a couple weeks when my family got a phone call saying that pictures had been recovered of the awful things that had been done to me and my name was on them. I hadn't told yet what had happened, so it was very traumatic being asked all sorts of questions by my family. I felt so ashamed. I had to fly out to Las Vegas where the incidents had taken place to testify. I was so scared that I would be hurt by the man who abused me if I told in front of him. The day before the trial they took me into the courtroom to make it seem "not so scary" for the next day. As soon as I sat down I started bawling. I was overwhelmed with terror of sitting on that stand. I had been taught a lot about Christianity and I had come to believe in God. That night I prayed that I wouldn't have to testify. I just kept asking God over and over in my head. The next day I was still praying, yet everyone around me kept telling me I was going to have to go to the court room and tell them my story. About an hour before I was to go to the court room I went in to take a shower. When I came out from the bathroom clean, dressed and ready, they told me my assailant had taken a plea bargain. Apparently the attorneys had been trying to convince him of taking it for some time, and that morning he went to his lawyer and said he would do it. I definitely believe that God and the angels had everything to do with this change.

—Anita Helton, Student, Author
anitahelton@gmail.com
West Palm Beach, Florida

Small Requests are Important Too

When my daughter was young we talked about angels a lot. I always said no matter how small your request may seem, all you have to do is ask them to help you. As a baby I noticed that she was not kicking straight out with both legs. Immediately I consulted her doctor. After a lot of tests she was diagnosed with polio. We were so glad to see however, that as she grew one leg was only a little shorter than the other. She had a slight limp and grew tired quicker than her sister.

As a result she wasn't able to play sports. Yet as she grew up very few people noticed that she had the limp. She went to college, but although she wasn't able to play in any sports, she decided to join a gym. Her choice was to take a class in Spinning. This can be a strenuous exercise. The day after her first class she called me and said how difficult it was for her to finish the class, but she remembered our talks about Angels and how they would always help if you asked. She then said "Angels I need your help. Please let me be strong enough to finish this exercise." She told me, "Mom, it was as if I became 10 times stronger than when I started the class."

This seemed like a little thing when you think what miracles Angels can perform, but to her it was proof that Angels will help any time you ask.

—Sally M. Basso, CSC
Higher Connections Hypnotherapy, Astrology
Hypnobasso@verizon.net
McLean, Virginia

Angels Blessing

Big Dreams!

In January 1995, I wondered what it would be like to meet actor, Brad Pitt. What would it be like to work along side him or to have a conversation with him. I knew that I had angels around me and I knew everyone has angels around them, so Brad Pitt would as well. I also knew I could talk to my angels and they could talk with Brad's angels and maybe get things rolling. So, I asked my angels to please talk to Brad Pitt's angels and if at all possible that our paths would cross one day. The next morning I received a phone call from my best friend. She was so excited! She told me that there had been an announcement on the radio that morning saying Brad Pitt would be doing a movie in the area. I couldn't believe my ears. So I told her what I had done with my angels the night before and we just thought," Wow, the angels work fast!" Now there is a 50/50 chance that I will meet Brad Pitt. At the time, I worked as a promoter with unsigned bands. Our soundman and I had some downtime at a show and he proceeded to tell me that he also works in film production. He mentioned to me that a movie is coming into town and I should send my resume. He continued to nudge me about sending the resume to his contact. I finally decided to fax it. The next day I received a phone call. I was offered an internship because all the paying positions were taken. What an experience! I worked along side an academy award winning set decorator, production director and actors. Who would have thought it possible? The angels of course! I eventually was offered a paying position on the movie and the rest is history. Sing the praises of angelic synchronicity in your life. You never know what the Universe and your angels may place in your path to help you create your heart's desire. Go with spirit and enjoy the journey! Dream big!

—Sally Boccella Bates, ATP, CM
Angelic Connection
www.AngelicConnection.com
Raleigh, North Carolina

Blessed by an Angel

On October 29th, 2006 my daughter Justine will be thirty years old. Here is how I was introduced to her Spirit. My former wife Connie and I were practicing Rosicruicans, and living in Las Palmas de

Gran Canaria in the Canary Islands when we determined to give life to a child. In accordance with teachings we held sacred, we made love once per month at the most fertile moment to conceive, and we did.

We lived high in the sky on the 11th floor of the lovely Edificio Cantabria with balconies facing both puertas and beaches. I often spent time late at night watching the port, and one such night a bright light, brilliant beyond compare, arose on my balcony and followed me inside. I had been taught to not be afraid of such manifestations, but to greet the Spirit and ask what it wanted, why it was visiting.

I did and it said to me, Angel as it was, "I am the unborn Spirit of your child, the baby that is growing inside the sleeping body of my mother in the adjacent bedroom. I came to greet you and tell you I have selected you to be my parents." I replied how happy I was to see her and know her in this special way, and in a brief moment, she was gone. As I tell this story to others who are wise in spiritual matters they always reply it is not unusual for such things to happen. Nevertheless, I feel very blessed by this event as it is the only time I have ever seen an Angel, although I know they are in fact all around us.

—James B Rose, MPT
www.iTitanium.com
Wildwood Crest, New Jersey

Angels Listening

A Special Gift

I was given the gift of a four leaf clover several years ago. My friend had spotted it at a local park while we were talking. It was handed to me along with a wish for good luck. I graciously accepted it, tucking the clover away in a book that I later preserved as a special token of our friendship.

A year or so later, I had thoughts of throwing my gift into the garbage. Our friendship had dwindled, and I decided I was moving on. I didn't need any reminders of what once was because it didn't exist anymore. I can only recall considering throwing it out; I don't remember actually doing it.

Time passed and we reconciled our differences, remaining in touch on occasion. We shared a bond that kept our hearts connected. We leaned on each other during difficult times. Comfort and smiles were only a phone call away when needed, and I thought it would be this way forever.

When least expected, my friend passed away very suddenly. In shock the grief I felt was overwhelming.

My heart was heavy with a sadness I had never experienced before. I felt lost, not knowing what to do with myself. It was on my mind continually how I would heal without the help of my friend. Then I remembered the clover, that simple gift from one heart to another! I searched everywhere, tearing my home upside down and inside out trying to find this gift. I couldn't remember if I had in fact thrown it out. I prayed that I hadn't done it—that was unthinkable! I asked God and the Angels to help me find it.

It didn't take me long to realize that it was likely I had discarded this very special gift. So, I began frequenting my yard in search of a replacement. I needed something I could look at, something I could hold in my hand. I was looking for comfort and it nearly became an obsession that carried on for months. Then one day Spirit told me to "stop looking! You are clinging to the past and this is not good for you! When you are at peace with yourself, you will be given another four leaf clover as a gift."

With that message from Spirit, I did my best to let go of my obsession. I began to relax a little. Reality was sinking in. My friend was gone, and there was no replacing someone so special with a "thing". All that was left was for me to make peace with the loss and let my heart swell with love as it did before— before I felt the depth of grief I was now experiencing.

Five months later (to the day of hearing Spirit's message), I was cleaning up my yard. I casually walked around the budding trees and the edges of my flower beds. It was a perfect day to clear away the winter debris and prepare for the beauty of springs breathtaking blooms. As I headed toward the trash with my hands full of twigs, I admired the buds emerging on my favorite Irises. I could hardly wait to see their gorgeous purple blooms! I stopped and leaned over to get a good look at the buds—there were so many! Then my eye caught sight of it, a beautiful four leaf clover that was peaking out just beneath the green foliage. A smile came over my face and my heart raced with excitement. I had come a long way in the last year. I was more at peace than I had been in a very long time This was my sign from God, the Angels and heaven! My prayers were heard and answered! My heart was filled with such gratitude and joy. I kept thinking "Wow! This is so amazing!" Little did I know that there was more to this gift. Within inches of that clover, I soon discovered two more! The number three has always been significant to me. It means "I love you". My heart swelled bigger as I realized I was experiencing multiple signs and miracles, courtesy of my Angels! I couldn't have imagined this happening to me in a more perfect way! Thank you, Angels! I love you too!

It was a glorious experience finding the clovers. Each one is beautiful, unique and precious. But what I treasure the most is the gift of knowing that I received that day. With the help of my Angels, I know that I am loved—without a doubt!

—D.S., USA

Brave Soldier

Sergeant Major Linda Kay Torres Henderson was my husband's sister. She served our country for 28 years. She became ill with incurable cancer and left us on September 15, 2002. The evening of September 14th, I had gone to visit my grandchildren and watch movies with them. I came home about midnight to find my husband sleeping in the living room with all the lights turned off. I asked him why he was sleeping sitting up on the couch. He told me he had been praying to all the angels that I have all around my living room. He stated that after I had left to see my grandchildren, he received a call from his brother-in-law to invite him to come over and watch the boxing matches. He had listened to the message but decided not to answer the phone. He then looked at all the angels in the room and asked them to please go and be with his sister Linda, for he wanted angelic comfort for her. He then looked at Archangel

Michael and asked him to go and take his sister to heaven so that she wouldn't have to suffer anymore with this disease. He told Archangel Michael that his sister was also a soldier like him and to please take her to God. At 3:00 a.m. we received a call from my husband's other sister informing us Linda had passed. His sister later told us before she had passed Linda was sitting at the edge of the bed watering beautiful flowers and his sister had asked her to lie down. Soon Linda got back upon the bed and said she was leaving. His sister asked her where was she going and Linda said she was going home. Archangel Michael heard his plea and took it to God, and it was answered.

—Caroline Lara, ATP
carolangelites@yahoo.com
Houston, Texas

Dear Angels

I had seen Dr. Virtue a few times and taken some of her workshops. When I heard about the ATP course for certification being offered in Miami in 2001, I was really drawn to it. The problem was I did not have the money and no prospects for it. But I had learned from Doreen to give my desire to the angels to take care of for me. I said something like "Dear

Angels, I know that if I am meant to be there you will find a way for me." I was also apprehensive because my mom was very ill at the time and I was at her bedside every minute when I was not working. A day or two later I got a call from someone I met in Pittsburgh, PA at one of Doreen's seminars. We only met each other "by accident" in the lunch line, but felt we knew each other. She said "Jo Ann, I know this is a rough time for you right now (I was also going through a difficult divorce at the time), but I was wondering if you'd like to attend the ATP course with me in Miami. I will pay for the entire thing. My husband and I would prefer that I do not travel alone." I just couldn't believe the way the Angels worked in my life. I am forever grateful for them, and plan to continue working with them in service to others for the rest of my life.

—Jo Ann Kist, ATP
joangel444@yahoo.com
Akron, Ohio

Afterword

With every book I write, it is always my heartfelt desire that when you've finished reading the book you have expanded your thoughts, heart, and spiritual awareness so that you raised your vibration to a higher level. As you raise your vibration higher and higher, you allow more love to flow. When love flows from within you, your life becomes extraordinary as you create the desires of your heart into the reality of your life. *That is my heart's desire for you!*

The voice of an angel is the voice of love. Love heals everything as it creates from a place of perfection and abundance. The angels are love expressing from the light of God. There is no greater love than this and it comes to you as a gift, freely given, if you simply ask. As you've read these stories of the powerful angelic assistance that was given freely to so many people in all walks of life, I truly hope you begin right now by calling on the angels to assist you as you continue on your life journey. They will assist you in more ways than you can imagine and will always help to raise your vibration into a greater awareness of love. It's beautiful in that place, and with the angels by your side,

you can make your life into anything you dream it could be.

The angels want you to have your dreams fulfilled. They await your call so they can bring these dreams into your reality. It makes them excited and happy to bring miracles into your life and watch you smile. This is their calling—to assist you on your life journey so that you experience love, peace and joy. The experiences of angelic encounters shared in this book are available for you too. Simply ask my friend, and the sky will seemingly open for you!

As I close this book, I'm leaving you with a story from my life that transformed me so profoundly there is no earthly vocabulary to accurately portray what I experienced.

In March, 2000, I visited a practitioner who has multiple spiritual gifts, one of which is helping people release buried hurts and memories. I deeply admire this person and was guided to take advantage of some sessions with him. After the release session was completed, he left the room as meditation music played softly so I could remain in that cleansed, quiet state. I was in no way expecting what occurred.

I could hear the angels calling me, telling me to come see them in the light. It felt as if they were touching me, taking my hand, and encouraging me to follow. There were many around me and I began to feel my spirit lifting up out of my body, slipping away into the ethereal light. I felt lost in spaciousness. I was floating and in a split second I went through clouds and sky and saw a dazzling white light, so bright I thought it would blind me. Yet I saw clearly and everything was sparkling like gems reflecting the rays of the sun. There was no awareness of space or time. I panicked. What was happening to me? Where was I? With a jolt I was back in my body, but a moment later I floated again toward the ethereal light. This happened one more time before I realized my fear was making me return to my body, and I strongly wanted to go back to the beautiful light.

My third attempt took me fully into the light. My first guardian angel Hope was standing there with her massive wings spread in magnificent splendor. Her garment was a silvery blue that sparkled and her blue eyes seemed to dance in the brilliant light. She was breathtakingly beautiful! As Hope grasped my hand I felt a magnificent surge of overwhelming love pulse through me. I felt as if I was melting into a pile as a snowman does when the sun rises in the sky; I couldn't comprehend the feeling it was so electrifying. She simply said, "You made it. I'm so glad you are here.

We have much to share with you." As I glanced to the left I saw my dad. He approached me to hug me, except it wasn't an earthly embrace of bodies touching, it was the surrounding of light filled with love. He was glowing and although he looked as he did on earth, his face looked smooth, no aging lines; he looked like a younger version of when I last saw him on earth. We exchanged some words then my grandparents appeared as did various people who had been in my life for a time, but had left already. It was so amazing; they just appeared instantaneously. Somehow they would enter my thoughts and immediately they were in front of me. Then I recognized them, walking towards me, but yet how could I since I'd never seem them on earth. My two other children, who left my womb before their birth, were standing in front of me and I knew them, a girl and a boy, just as I'd always known somewhere deep inside of me. We embraced but again there was no sense of bodily forms touching, only the uniting of spirits and a profound sensation of love that flooded me as oneness with all that is. Then I glanced in the distance and saw a brilliant light blazing with intensity moving toward me.

The light was so bright with beams radiating in every direction; the form had outstretched arms, and then *in an instant the form was in front of me. Like a cloud suddenly lifting, I recognized the form as Jesus. So much love poured out from him and his eyes were soft, twinkling as he smiled at me. His countenance was pure love and I marveled at his smile, not somber in his expression as was often depicted on earth. Holding out his hands and taking mine in his he simply said, "Welcome child." At that moment I cannot put into words the feeling of love that surged through me. It was more than my being could hold and I began to tremble from the ecstasy of it. We began to walk and Hope joined us on my other side. Here I was, walking in the light between Jesus and my first guardian angel Hope!*

We were walking as we do on earth but there was no contact by my feet; it seemed as if we were gliding in air. The path appeared to be glass, yet it was soft and warm and mirrored our feet while at the same time our feet, like shapes of light, appeared to go beneath as in a three-dimensional, unexplainable mystery— totally amazing. So much color was around me, vibrant shades of the entire universal spectrum of color. Angels were everywhere and they were clad in garments of vibrant color. Some were adorned in white but most glowed with the vibrancy of color; only the light that glowed around them was a bril-

liant white haze. Mountains graced the background with astonishing hues of rich purples and blues and the fields below were the greenest green I'd ever seen. Birds flew right up to me and seemed to be looking me in the eyes as if they knew me and were greeting me. The angels were busy in a flurry of activity but everything was in total peace. Strains of the most beautiful musical sounds came to my ears, as a choir singing with unusual instruments accompanying them. It was the most harmonious blend of the purest sound, something I'd never heard before.

Buildings stood beyond me and seemed to glow. I noticed animals scampering and playing in the distance while lions walked calmly beside the lambs. Everywhere I looked there was only love, peace and harmony. Beautiful waterfalls flowed over rocks and small hills, flowing into streams with the clearest water ever beheld by my eyes. All was in perfect order. We came to an archway arrayed with green foliage and lush orchid type flowers cascading profusely over this arch, but the arch had nothing supporting the flowers; it just remained suspended there, like magic. Huge blooms in many colors of flowers surrounded the benches they motioned for me to sit on, but as I approached the bench it seemed to be only light. However, the bench held us, I guess because we were *spirits, and spirits don't need any form on which to sit. Jesus turned to me and said "You are troubled. You have questions to ask of me."*

For some time I had been given the knowledge through others and my own angelic messages that I had heal-ing work to do. My money was tight and I was unsure as to what trainings or classes I should take to gain the proper tools to do this, and I knew I had to be selective because of my budget. I had done research and at times thought about taking a particular class, but nothing ever seemed "right." I was puzzled, for how could I do the work if I wasn't trained? This was my perception. Some practitioners had suggested Reiki or something similar and mentioned I needed an attunement to do healing work. So I asked Jesus, "I need to know which training I should take in order to do my work. You know about my funds, so which is the best one for me to take and also receive my attunement?"

With that Jesus took my hands in his and looking deeply into my eyes as if he knew everything about me, expressing so much love and kindness as he said in his gentle voice, "All you ever need is within you. Here is your attunement. Now you must go and do your work." At that moment an overwhelming surge of love swept through me with such force that I felt as if I my heart would explode. I felt connected with the whole of my beingness. There was no separation; I was aware of my body but I didn't feel in it. Tears sprang with a gush from the center of my being through my eyes; I couldn't absorb it all. I was looking down and experiencing sensations of my physical body at the same time. I felt as if I was bursting and couldn't contain the love that engulfed me, for I was one with the Divine essence of love. It was a moment in which the love and what I was feeling transcended my form and being, and gave me a glorious glimpse of the perfect universal love and power of the spirit realm.

Hope smiled and I knew I never wanted to leave this place. Knowing my thoughts, Jesus said, "You must go back for you have much to do. Your mission has just begun and the world needs what you have to give. You must go for your time is not yet Dear One. You can come back, but your purpose is on earth right now." With that Jesus vanished and Hope guided me to the place where I had entered the light. She embraced me and with a thought I was back on the table in my practitioner's room.

My body was heavy and I couldn't move. My fingers felt swollen and enlarged; I couldn't move them either. I felt weighted down, glued to the table, but at the same time weightless, not even real. Yet I knew I was present in that room. Ever so slowly I came back into full awareness of my surroundings in physical form. The practitioner came back into the room as he heard my sobs, the tears continuing to flow from deep within me. I knew I'd never be the same again. The practitioner sat down beside me and asked if I wanted to talk. I shared some but was almost speechless. How could I put into words what I had just experienced? Somehow I knew he believed me and knew I had just experienced something beyond the normal understanding of our natural world. I traveled to the light several more times over the next few weeks, and each one was a glorious phenomena.

Was it a dream? Did I make it all up? They were my first thoughts, but I knew it was real. I was there. I felt the love that goes beyond anything comprehendible in this world. No words could ever adequately describe my experience. Yes, it was real and my life transformed into something extraordinary from that day forward.

And so it is…

About the Author

Carolyn Porter, D. Div., an internationally known teacher, spiritual counselor, wholeness coach and channel for the angels, is totally guided and inspired in her life by the realm of the angels, archangels and ascended masters.

Carolyn holds a Doctorate and Masters of Divinity, and a B.S. in Music Education. She is the owner of Empower Productions, Inc., co-founder and co-owner of the All About Health store, and recently opened her own healing center in Woodstock, Georgia—Where Miracles Happen.

Porter's books and insights have been shared on radio and in magazines throughout the United States, and she continues to offer hope to those who seek a better life through her workshops, trainings, books, audios and angel sessions. To sign up for Carolyn's free enewsletter, receive her free ebook, or contact her for a personal session, visit www.drcarolynporter.com.

Carolyn resides in Woodstock, Georgia, a northern suburb of Atlanta.

Suggested Reading

Archangels and Ascended Masters by
Doreen Virtue, Ph.D.

Angel Numbers by Doreen Virtue, Ph.D.

Angel Visions I and II by Doreen Virtue, Ph.D.

The Angelspeake Storybook by Barbara Mark
and Trudy Griswold

Your Guardian Angels by Linda Georgian

Angel Medicine by Doreen Virtue, Ph.D.